A
Poetry Archive

Volume 5
Conversations, Mythologies
and Foreign Voices
2010–2013

Frank Prem

Wild Arancini Press
2024

Publication Details

Title: A Poetry Archive Archive Volume 5:
Conversations Mythologies and Foreign Voices — 2010 - 2013

ISBN: 978-1-923166-39-4 (p-bk)
ISBN: 978-1-923166-36-3 (e-bk))

Published by Wild Arancini Press
Copyright © 2025 Frank Prem
All rights reserved:

No part of this publication may be reproduced, stored in a retrieval system, or transmitted in any form or by any means, electronic, mechanical, photocopying, recording or otherwise, without prior written permission from the publisher and author.
A catalogue record for this book is available from the National Library of Australia.

Cover Image: Wild Arancini Press

*And still, wherever I look . . .
there lies my story*

CONTENTS

A Poetry Archive Volume 5

Introduction 1

2010 (Part 1) 3

2010 (Part 2) 53

2011 99

2012 (Part 1) 137

2012 (Part 2) 159

Joseph Cambell - Mythology 181

In a Foreign Tongue 207

After Words 243
    Index of Poems 245
    Author Information 251
    Other Published Works 253
    What Readers Say 255

A Poetry Archive Volume 5

Introduction

The A *Poetry Archive* series captures the great majority of poetic work undertaken by Frank Prem and not published in dedicated collections elsewhere.

The current collection (*Volume 5*) continues the reorientation of Prem's writing to a more direct communication with the reader incorporating the more conversational tone that has become characteristic of his later work.

Volume 5 captures work undertaken during 2010 - 2013, and includes random poetry, a fresh interpretations of mythologiccal themes inspired by readings of the work of mythologist Joseph Campbell, as well as work undertaken in two languages to reflect an undertsanding of immigrants to Australia froma particular time period.

Each poem a universe, complete.

2010 (Part 1)

2010 (Part 1)

getting on (I said getting on)

I have learned I must repeat
most things I say

> *I said*
> *I have learned to repeat*
> *most of what I say*

it's nobody's fault
just the way things turn out
when one of us is deaf
or chronically inattentive

> *I said*
> *it's not your fault*

I wonder sometimes
if silence would be better
endless repetition often makes the meaning
obsolete
but we persevere
with our circuitous linguistic patterning
of call and response

> *I said*
> *we persevere don't we*

and we adjust through a long life
to all of each other's various flaws
and foibles

well
you have to if you want to survive

> *I said*
> *we get along all right*
> *don't we*
> *love*

decisive pastorale

the summer glows benign
from out of a blue-field sky
streaked with cloud floss
to leave a winged impression

the dog is on investigation
underneath a footbridge
that she's never found to be of interest
in the past

the waves of grass from spring
have begun to topple
in crop circles
randomly
everywhere

touches of green remain
among the gold that's started greying
rich and ripe
almost to the point of decay

and the sparrows
those township scavengers
have turned pastoral

all along the path
they're in the grass

rising here and there
to pause a moment
before a sudden dive
and subsequent disappearance

2010 (Part 1)

here a group of four
is holding conference
hovering in a circle to make plans

> *one is for the electrified fence*
> *to straddle in defiance*
>
> *two is off to sit within the tree*
>
> *three is waiting patiently*
> *for everyone else to decide*
>
> *but four has already gone*
> *down into the seedbeds*
> *of fallen grass*

who needs to make decisions
when the answers
lie scattered all around

this is honey-summer
under a blue-field sky
benign

maintaining equilibrium

tick

tock

tick

tock

he seems to be an ordinary
and unassuming little man

tick

wearing a checked flannel shirt
and a pair of worn blue jeans

tock

a workman's boots
and those long woollen socks

tick

the only thing that might be a bit odd
about him is his arm

tock

for it seems over-long
slightly disproportionate

tick

but I guess that's just the way
that he was made

tock

2010 (Part 1)

and he doesn't do a lot all day
but stand stooped to grasp behind him

    tick

I know because I've taken time
to watch him

    tock

but all through his immobility
the sound seems to echo around him

    tick

and the hand on the arm
that's stretched so far around

    tock

is wrapped around the key
click click he unwinds two turns

    tick

click click with a turn of the hand
he winds back up again

    tock

it seems unusual
but it's just his particular way

    tick

to maintain an elusive state
of equilibrium

    tock

a last vestige of magic

he lies on a hospital bed
on loan to his bedroom
at home

his brain is shot full of holes by now
like cheese
or a colander
straining the meaning out of his thoughts
but not large enough yet
to kill

and he mumbles to himself
while they wipe him down
strangers who rotate through in shifts
to bathe him
to feed him
to wash his backside when he shits

he makes hardly any sense at all
and I can understand just one word
or two
in maybe twenty

then he opens his eyes wide
round
fixes a stare on me
and grasps my warm hand
with his own chilly claw

and speaks
in a voice
that can only have been channeled
direct from god

> I am a Carer
> I can make you better
> I said
> I am a Carer
> and I can send you Home

2010 (Part 1)

do you believe

*you have to believe
and then I can send you
Home*

he lies back
mumbling again
while they finish their malodorous tasks

I can mostly understand
just a single word
or two
in perhaps twenty

      ... Carer ...

      ...make you well ...

      ...believe me dad ...

      ...you must ...

      ...send you Home ...

      ... believe ...

stars of the in-crowd

the stars are flying north
and east and west
and everywhere I look
they are leaving

there will come a day
when the sky up there
is painted only black
no spots of flicker-white
left anywhere

I guess it is *the bang*
they are still running from
the sight and sound of heat and light
and the crowded place
so suddenly crammed
inside a moment
of time

2010 (Part 1)

hurrah for the salt

when I smell the briny sea
I start walking with a rolling gait
as though I was a sailor-man
with a boat beneath my feet

> *hurrah hurrah for the sea and the tar*
> *hurrah for the able seaman*
> *hurrah hurrah there's rum in the jar*
> *and hurrah for the salt I'm breathing*

when I come near the fish-laden air
I start testing the breeze for squalls
as though I held a wheel in my hands
and all hands a-waiting my call

when I hear the white gulls cry
beneath my feet I feel the planking
as though I stood on a deck worn smooth
by storm-wash and wave-spanking

when I cast my eye over harboured boats
I hear the ropes and wires singing
and I feel as though there's sea in my veins
with a fair wind in my rigging

> *so hurrah hurrah for the rum in my jar*
> *hurrah for the waters green I'm dreaming*
> *hurrah hurrah for the sea and the tar*
> *and hurrah for the salt hurrah*

The season of waiting

The summer we waited for the boy to slip away was a sweltering dampness that held us somehow out of place. A pocket of temperate tropicality about a million miles from any meaningful equator.

That season was a succession of thunders and intense light displays, with never a let-up in the sticky heat. Uncomfortable, itching days and hot drowning nights, while the gods toyed idly with us, and threw dice to determine his fate.

It was not all bleak, no. The garden throve in the humid embrace and vines slithered relentlessly into and out of each available crack and crevice. Fruit appeared, minute on one day, grotesquely pendulous on the next.

Radiant colour seemed to erupt from the flowers and yet, with each storm front that built and sucked the air from our atmosphere, the feeling was that of a brooding hulk bearing down with an indifferent determination, arisen from somewhere above and beyond this minor playing board and these minor pieces.

In our different ways we shared a sense that this season would be the culmination, and that both trivia and meaning should be set to one side, could wait for another turn, yet only incessant heat and the oppressive thunder, pressure and portent, lingered for day after day, with no relief through rain.

A thin-waisted wasp spent *her* days busy, building an elaborate multi-chambered nest, bigger than my opened hand. Each chamber filled with a stunned spider and a voracious grub. All the time she added: new chambers, new spiders, new grubs. Life and death lying, side by side but invisible, plastered over by the shaped mud of the wasp's work.

Of course, he wasn't really a boy.

2010 (Part 1)

The term was just a hangover from long-ago habit, but in an odd way the stricken don't seem to age in the same sequence that others of us do, they become instead chronologically frozen at the point when youth was taken from them.

There was no ease to be found that summer. We, all of us, felt the sticky discomfort every day while we waited on the random cast of a die, and for the rain to fall.

Radiance after

After the storm, before the air had cleared of the belaboring humidity and while the sensation of physical pressure still lingered, nothing seemed quite as it was meant to be.

The displacement emphasised by the mist-blurred trees of our streetscape as the wind moaned and whistled, dogging the progress of the billowing discontent that fumed overhead.

We had clung to the prospect of a change with disproportionate hope, as though the passage of mere weather could force relief of those other stresses as well.

In the aftermath, with the atmosphere returned to a less charged, less urgent normality, there was almost the sense of being let down, for there was no resolution at all, but more the sense that we had been abandoned, to do as we would in the best ways we knew how until the barometer rose yet again.

The downpour had left the outside world clean, smelling of wellness. Of rightness. Everything had been enlivened and radiance was the only apt word term to come to mind, dismissed immediately with what was now an inbuilt lack of trust, and reluctance to accept seemingly good things at their face value.

The old story tells that Lazarus returned from the dead, but was it ever proven that he actually died first?

It was hard to believe that the boy had *come good*.

Hard to conceive such a deliverance – if that is what it was. Certainly it was no reprieve, only a failure to execute the sentence – for the moment.

to start the day

beneath the hot rush of shower water
he rubs
timidly
at the angry flesh of his legs and torso

winces at instant feedback
brought on in reaction
to an almost addictive need
to manually rid himself
of this florid emanation
that he sees as a kind of stigmata

water turned off
he stands clutching the damp towel
to his face
and imagines tears

imagines holding his own precious psyche
inside himself
lest it abandon him forever
in response to his failure to achieve
an unstated moral standard
innate and instinctive

eventually the steam-mist clears
even for him
and he is able to complete the task

make the necessary adjustments
to coif and attire
mentally put aside the burning discomfort
of his irritated skin
and proceed into the day

what the tiler saw

the tiler on the estate at Melton Hills
has laid oven-baked terra cotta today

tomorrow will be imported squares
from Italy

fossils in the slate take him
on a journey to the past
among strange fish that swam
through rocky seas

and the patterns on the brown blocks
in a bathroom were shaped like faces
in one of them he saw *her* eyes
and paused

how can the random lines
in powder-coated clay
recall the image of someone he once knew
so well

why couldn't they just be fishes
in a swell

mathematics and philosophy

nobody can live your life
except for you
nobody else can do
the things you'll do

but when you find yourself
wondering
who to be
it might be mathematics
that can set you free

just remember
division makes you smaller than you realise
and subtraction leaves you
nothing but your pride
addition will still want doing
after every meal
and exponential multiplication is bigger . . .

much bigger
than it feels

the memory-keepers of april

and in the morning
we saw them all

>*shining medals*
>*fresh-pressed khaki*

each at a kind of attention
while the bugle sounded
one more last post

weary old survivors
with eyes closed
to recall sharp-witted boys
assembled in regimental lines
of slouched cigarettes
and felted hats

those remembered faces
still hold the look of home
of small towns
and wide bush stations
but the beautiful fresh bodies
always fall in those same bloody ways
into mud

and into the shroud
of fog and smoke

the light dim
on the rising sons
of an expeditionary force
that never have grown old

dividing the labour

Franklin, I'm waiting.
Won't you come and fetch the water?

> *Well, all right, just a second,*
> *the news is showing on the TV.*

You've been procrastinating,
come and do the things you ought to.

> *I heard you bellow and beckon.*
> *I'll be there when you see me.*

Franklin, you've got work to do.

> *Mother, I've got things to do.*

inadequate staves

Avast there, you staves,
you best quaver before my crotchet,
for there'll be minim rest
for you!

Come on, my hearties, beat!
Yes, beat – four to the bar!
Three to the bar!
Two to the bar!

Again!

Again!

You hollow looking groupers,
what's with your long tails?
Are you all flat,
or only semibreve?

Hey there, sharpen up!
I don't care for your semi-tones
or your treble-ings.

Black notes, ahoy!

universe smiles

when he closed his eyes to sleep
the stars appeared
and through the night
they twinkled and shone

a slow pirouette
danced around the darkness
by glittering sequins
arrayed across the sky

and in his dream
he smiled

~

when he opened his eyes
awake
the sun was there
golden upon the blue
that became day

the warmth as it touched him
brought a kick of pleasure

his hands waved
trying to catch the light

he gurgled in joy

and through the waking hours
he laughed

the boy bands of palestine

*I do not like the jesus band
they make me feel uncomfortable*

*their main one
I generally found to be acceptable
he sang well
as though he knew the songs
both words and meaning
and it was for him
I came today to listen*

*but it seems he has been removed
and another –
a less compelling performer –
is trying to be the lead singer*

*in the old arrangement
this group sounded well
quite compelling sometimes
but now their vocals are much too falsetto*

*always tremolo
and more tremolo*

*the harmonies are sweet
but they grate on me*

*and my leg
well my leg is healed it is true
but it feels wrapped in sugar
as though it is whole
yet rotting inside*

*it is somehow
un-trustable*

2010 (Part 1)

and you know I have been told –
in whispers only –
of other bands
who sing deeper
with more body
tenor voices and bass
but I am not allowed to hear them

like they have sung a spell into me
I am prevented

ach
here comes Peter and his group again
crooning as though there is nothing
more pleasing to the ear
in the whole world

but this leg aches I tell you
it seems whole
but it is unsound

almost
I could wish I were lame again
almost that I had never heard
of the miracle songs

pah
would that I could stopper
my ears

plays pictures

every brush stroke
is a note

each new colour
note to *chord*

and she plays
an idea into life

and she brushes
chord to melody

why do I —
when I look into her picture —
want to sing

why do I —
when I hum a simple bar or two —
find images
dancing inside my head

as she builds the painting
the song will rise and fall

fall and rise

until the canvas holds
vibration
stilled to reflect life

she plays pictures
rise and fall

she paints music
fall and rise

2010 (Part 1)

just shopping

he misses her in the supermarket

finds himself buying things
he never would have bought alone
hydroponic tomatoes
recycled paper
for the smallest room

there is no one to laugh with

he forgot the carry-bag from home again . . .

ah well that's the way it goes
with the environment

everyone's intentions are good

how is it
that holding hands in the aisle

> *where the butter is spreadable*
> *and the cold comes from the cool chests*
> *that store yoghurt*
> *(he really almost bought yoghurt)* . . .

how is it that it seems ok

it was never so *ok* before

he misses her
and stocking up is just a chore

but sometimes
when he wheels the trolley around a corner
he can picture the selection
of fruit or veg
and it's enough to make him stop

a nuisance to people
who just want to get on
with shopping

the simple life

let love bless this simple life I live
in the beauty of the sunrise at its dawning
and may love bless
the simple things that are my gifts
the rising sound of song
that fills each morning

I stand upon the green grass
cast my eye upon the field
contemplate the rows I laid
the seed I've not yet spilled

I picture what will one day be
in the places I've prepared
picture bliss within my mind
and find myself right there

so let love bless my simple life
beauty beneath the sky
let love bless these simple things
the song that rises high

growing season

another crop is almost in the ground
potato eyes have almost popped
and they're all waiting round
to harden

the mulch is mixed
the straw is piled up high
later on there may be rain falling
gently from the sky
on our garden

this is spring
this is the season
to grow
this is spring
this is the reason we sow

this is spring
these are the days
when everything seems to know

this is the time to grow

bees are calling apples into bloom
pumpkin seeds are running wild
and taking all the room
no begging pardon

the rhubarb's slow
might need another year
but our leeks have shot to heaven
in the higher stratosphere
of our garden

this is spring
this is the season
to grow
this is spring
this is the reason we sow

this is spring
these are the days
when everything seems to know

it is time to grow

time to grow

mary's sideboard

if you take out the sideboard
then run it down to mary's
you can use all your bylines
and a word you wrote contrary
to vault inside her window
taking aim for glass or glory
but turn down your within-glow
on a long-hand-written story

then come home
then come home

mary was a wrangling queen
who fell out with her father
when he said *a-hey-ni-hey-hey*
in a most offensive manner
that upset the keeling balance
of a spirit lit by falling stars
that spluttered for just a moment
of dis-ori-ent-ation

all alone
all alone

but mary mary will you dance tonight
the moon is shining and the stars are bright
I'll trip you a reel with your feet in flight
and by morning we'll be home

and mary mary will you dance with me
the moon and the stars will play for free
I'll spin you around with a *fiddle-de-de*
and by morning we'll be home

in the morning I'll bring you home
in the morning I'll bring you home

if you ever pass your way-breath
in the district of el-faren
you'll see mary flying free-wheel
on a foremost breezer blowing
and you'll pause for just a moment
find a way to ride the storm out
then turn your heart-boat higher
and remember what's been offered

then go home
then go home

but mary mary will you dance tonight
the moon is shining and the stars are bright
I'll trip you a reel with your feet in flight
and by morning we'll be home

and mary mary will you dance with me
the moon and the stars will play for free
I'll spin you around with a *fiddle-de-de*
and by morning we'll be home

in the morning I'll bring you home
in the morning I'll bring you home

in johnny's hat

down by the lake
I saw a girl in a boat
and a man in a hat like john's

his hand was on the tiller
hers was pulling on a line
if she had a fish
I couldn't really tell
but I wished her well at the time

then the man in the hat like john's
made a move
and the motor coughed
a little *per-per-pooh*

so the girl
and the line
and the hat like john's
put-putted their boat along

I almost called *hey johnny*
I almost hailed to him out loud
but in the nick of time
from the corner of my eye
I saw the real john
looking like he'd lost his hat
and scratching his head
on the corner

theme song

I don't sell my soul
to every passing stranger
though there's times I find myself
wishing that I could

and I don't bend low
I don't bow before danger
I put my back to the wall
when anyone says I should

there's just me all alone
with these few things I own
my heart and my soul
and some far-distant goal
that I can hardly see

it's lonely here sometimes
with so little to call mine
this life exacts a toll
but I gladly bear it all
to stay free

hic-atoo

>*hep*
>*scraa-ak*
>
>*hep*
>*scraa-ak*

some of it sounds familiar
scraa-ak is the love call
of the yellow-crested lothario
and his tribe but
hep . . .

that's a new one

I scour the trees

>*hep*
>*scraa-ak*

not in the eucalypts
to the south

>*hep*
>*scraa-ak*

not in the wattles
by the creek

>*hep*
>*scraa-ak*

there —
in the silky oak
dangling from the top branch
just above the last orange flower —
is the all-white screecher

hep

I never knew that cockatoos

    scraa-ak

suffered hiccups

sourcing a recipe

he is surrounded by recipe books
but none of them will do

he goes online

to

> *southern cooking*
> *simply recipes*
> *food tzar*
> *cookbooksdotcom*
> *and bellaonline*

he types
rhubarb recipes
into the search box
to find them all

like old friends

here's one
posted to the archives
in two thousand and four

> *we think you'll like it*

what about *aubergine*
is it possible to *preserve*
a lemon . . .

why would he want to

> *plum good cake*
> *pumpkin soup*

he can bake biscuits now
found out how
on a world-wide search

thank you *stella-three*
and *stefanie-number-one*

thank you *byron-the-cook*
for your tip
about sweet corn

he has to go offline now
to check that the crumble in the oven
doesn't burn

bye bye so long
until next time

2010 (Part 1)

dash slap

    they are a privilege to read

she said

    you know I think your writing's fine
    but
    don't you think it might improve
    if you sometimes took the time
    to look over what you've done
    before you send it

    like just there . . .

    an unfortunate near rhyme
    you would have noticed
    if you'd waited a little while

    and
    well
    I know you're not too keen
    on punctuation
    but I'm sure that you'd apostrophise
    if you'd kept your finger off the button
    for a day or even
    one hour

    I am delighted to receive your mail

she said

    your newest lines and stanzas
    the journal of your life

    but the way you dash it off
    and then away . . .

    I see you only
    living in first-drafted form

*you are unpolished
unless I brush the obvious
to help you shine
like your mother might have done
when you were small
and I confess
I am uncomfortable in such a place*

*I am adverse —
so to say —
to the secondary muse-maternal role*

*it is wonderful
you write so well*

she said

perhaps you could . . .

more slowly

if it's really . . .

this time it could be the end of the earth
and I wish I'd turned the stove off

this time it's the end of the world
but I wanted finish ironing my work-shirts

this time if it's the end of the earth
and
I meant to change my underwear
if it is the end of the earth this time

I never thought
I never really thought that I would live
to be there

that kind

it's the kind of a sky
that might shoot it's stars
I've got my eye on the pointers
and the southern cross

maybe I should be watching out
for mars or for saturn

on a night like this
I think that anything can happen

and any of the stars might fall
yes
any old star at all

sacred priest

there's a sacred ibis
stalking my back yard
ever formal in his black and white

I can see him
in the priesthood
perhaps
supervising sacrifice

his commentary spare
and dry

kate mcgarrigle (is gone)

kate mcgarrigle is dead
kate mcgarrigle is dead

I for one will miss her
I for one will miss her

anna must harmonise alone from now on
yes anna must harmonise alone from now on

for kate mcgarrigle is gone
alas for kate mcgarrigle
she is gone

full and empty

when you are here
the smallness of the world
is a journey to the still point
that holds meaning

when you are gone
the emptiness of the world
is a relentless chaos
that lacks meaning

demonstrating dreary

the dog is in the third day of vigil

each day lying in isolation
in the sun
allowing both enthusiasm
and demand
to rest within her
in a kind of long-term storage

at night
she makes a circuit of the empty bed
pauses to gaze at it
half accusingly
then drops with a sigh
to settle in for the night

there is no mourning
for she demonstrates clear anticipation
of return in due course
but the wait
is dreary

on the cathedral corner

the gargoyle perched on a corner pipe
of the cathedral of scary creatures
looks familiar

the eyes protrude
the head is angled in the suggestive way
that brings to mind
something that I can't quite recall

it looms
with a particular malicious pleasure

if it had the power to move
it would be *tongue*
licking lips

it's colleagues on the gables
are run-of-the-mill unpleasant
but this one seems personal

for me

I think I'll take her off her perch
take her home to bed
wild and wicked
in the dark all things scare the same
and I am brave enough

I believe that I am brave enough
to hold on to a ghoulie-goyle
when she shows her teeth
so brightly for me
in the night

moo-pera

the air is filled with cows
lowing a song of yearning
each occupying one small quarter
of misery and woe

upraised voices sound —
call response and chorus —
un-coordinated

drone and bray
and bellow

songs of poor fortune
and ill-omen
hunger and desire

they are languid idle
desperate and needful
herd voices vying loud
to be loudest

to be the one
that called out first

yes the day is filled
with an air of cows
un-conducted
singing for their hay

2010 (Part 1)

to the desert in pursuit

the poem I didn't write today
is seated on a train
crossing the empty nullarbor
to a western destination

I'd meant to commit the words to paper
but the ticket said
right now
and the poem I had in my mind
had moved along

if I'd etched it out this morning
before the sun was up and high
it would have been on the page
by cup-of-tea

or
I could have fleshed it out right after lunch
but I began to wonder *why*
and before I'd thought it through
the afternoon was gone

and I might have written it in full
by evening
but when the pen came to my hand
that poem was an escapee

on the run
and by then
it was a long time gone

perhaps if I were to join it there
both of us might write
of trains that crossed the desert
through the red-eyed night

at least then the poem
that I never wrote
would amount to some useful lines

I've never crossed the nullarbor
have never gone that way
it's only for this poem
that I'm crossing it today

reflection (requiem)

all I have
is only what I've done

all I know
is now and then it's gone

all I am
is all that I have seen
is all that I have loved
is all that I have been

life has made
the shape within my arms

life has drawn
the lines upon my palms

who I'll be
a story that I shared
a memory that I loved
a journey that I dared

years grow shorter day by day
life grows precious as it fades

the wine glass almost empty
the river run to sea
the star returned to darkness
the silent place inside of me

2010 (Part 2)

breeze and leaf

the breeze is playing tease
with the last yellow leaf
clinging to the surety
of its branch

> *fly with me*
> *come fly*

the breeze speaks of journeys
and of distance
other trees
and warm green fields

> *fly with me*
> *come fly away*

and the flight is all tumult
and skelter
pell-mell and fury
until the ground

and yet
it *was* a journey
after all

at Gloria Jean's

Gloria Jean is a girl of sixteen
wearing a black bob

> *how are you sir*
> *were you the flat white*
> *the latte or the mocha*
> *with chocolate sprinkles*

she is wielding a metal jug
full of thermometer and milk
while she wipes down the steam pipe
on the coffee machine
with a squirt of steam to ensure
it's as clean as can be

everything is clean
down here at Gloria's

she is the manager of coffee
cake snacks and cool drinks
in neat rows in the chiller
smiles politely
while brushes at a strand of hair
too willing to get involved

and the customers
like me
are making chitty-chat on mobile phones
at tables

and burbling
at prams and the little kids
within them

the mother's club meets on Thursdays

at least
that's how it seems

2010 (Part 2)

there's a meeting of the gang
every Thursday
at Gloria Jean's

gregorian cats

    ahhh-ah-ahh-ah-a-ah-ahhhh
        ahhh-ah-ahh-ah-a-ah-ahhhh
            ahhh-ah-ahh-ah-a-ah-ahhhh
    ahhh-ah-ahh-ah-a-ah-ahhhh
        ahhh-ah-ahh-ah-a-ah-ahhhh
ahhh-ah-ahh-ah-a-ah-ahhhh
        ahhh-ah-ahh-ah-a-ah-ahhhh
ahhh-ah-ahh-ah-a-ah-ahhhh
    ahhh-ah-ahh-ah-a-ah-ahhhh
_{ahhhh} **merrowwrrrr!! phtttt!!!!! rwerwr phtttt!!!!!** _{ahhhh}

rwerrr

Belvedere

there's a man with a hat
he calls 'Belvedere'
proud with a wide brown brim

it's a hat that he seems
to fit like a glove
and it seems to quite like
fitting him

Lacking a start

I had an idea
a line of dancers linking arms
half facing forward
half pointed the other way
to the back

raising one foot in unison
to stamp
and to stamp
then starting a rotation
around the still point
of the earth

and as they trod
the earth was moved beneath their feet
began to spin
until it turned and it turned
while the dancers kicked
and stamped

I had an idea
for the revolution of the world
but I could not find the way
to set the thing
into motion

the light (I)

I am the light
that shines in your dreams
I am the rock
you can hold

I am the bird
who will lend you her wings

and I am your welcome
back home

on the milky sea

there is a tiny speck of boat
on the calm of a milky sea
that I am warming
to make my coffee

and as the current starts to move
beneath the surface
the little boat up-anchors
and begins to sail

around froth-and-bubble islands
that come and go in unexpected bursts
of the white
wrathing ire
that rises from below

the pleasure cruise is troubled
as the waves start to pitch and toss
up and down and up again
there is strife now brewing overboard

and the seas will rise
as milk seas must
when the fire down below
is burned too brightly

and today I must play the hero

to the rescue is my part
so it's *off the heat*
and *up the jug*
then into the cup I'll pour

alas
alas
I lost the boat

the cure
perhaps
was too drastic

2010 (Part 2)

it may be
that I swallowed it

perhaps
it was merely downed

either way no good came
for the speck of boat
a-sail on the milky sea

the good day

the little dog said

> today is a good day
> for barking
>
> rreough! rreough!

as she lay full stretch
in the aromatic herbs
beneath the sun

she kept an eye on the door
in case her mistress should appear
maybe
to go walking
or failing that
to throw the ball
for awhile

oh it's a grand day out in the sun
for barking

> rreough! rreough!

and to lie on the ground
on your back
with legs in the air

everybody in the universe
should have such a sunny day

out in the garden
when there's no better thing to do
than woof

> good-day

to the world

taking possession

and we have purchased land

it is ours
but not yet
sacred

to sanctify
we must walk to every corner

stand in contemplation
of *our* footprints
in *this* place

touch the soil
then move on

> *here*
> *it is the north east*
> *this aspect*
> *is the west*

and saying this
we claim as our own
each new direction

towards the sun of morning

> *this is mine*
> *it is me standing here*

towards the evening
from where
the darkness rises

> *I dedicate my self*

I will make my monuments
and my temples
and with every change I cause
I will grow
until we are the same

no boundary line exists
between me
and my heart

2010 (Part 2)

building

papa said

>   son
>   that's a great way to go
>   it's the way we used to do things
>   when I was the man
>
>   there's always someone to lay down
>   rules and regulations
>   someone who's built the thing better before
>
>   but when you mark down an outline
>   with your own ruler and pencil
>   sketch out the places
>   where each thing must go
>
>   then front up to some guy
>   who knows his way around
>   a hammer and nails
>
>   say
>   I want it done this way
>   like nobody's ever done
>   such a thing before
>
>   that's when you know
>
>   look at the scaffolding
>   watch the frame rise
>   walk around the spaces
>   where each wall must go
>
>   try to imagine
>   your feet near the fireplace
>   a book in your hand
>   and your bum in a chair
>
>   your heart is uprising
>   and your home
>   is nearly there

wild winter

wild winter blows
and bellows
its shrieks and susurrations
each by turn

tumbling down
the downpour is drops
and drips
spilled each upon the next
until the crowd is a righteous
cacophony of rain
striking against the glass in series
of *one one ones*
and taps and knocks
at the whim of the wind
of wild winter

un-rushing

> *howlong*
> *chiltern*
> *dederang*
> *rutherglen*
> *wangaratta*
> *tarrawingee*
> *glenrowan*
> *eldorado*

the wind said

> no

nearly blew us off the road

the trees
fell to the ground
to stop us
and to say

> *don't do what you'll regret*
> *don't rush to make mistakes*
> *wait*
>
> *things might yet grow better*

and when we turned around
they did

on the winter wire

each afternoon
as the shadows of middle-winter fell
to fade the day
the first little black birds
arrived to settle-in
on the wire

in ones and twos they came
jostling and chirping —
an entire flock —
socializing in the encroaching dusk

an overcoated man watched them
from across the street
fascinated by their habits and ways
often speculating to himself
about what might be communicated
through their chatter

he took to idly directing his thoughts
towards them as he watched
urging a particular idea
for this bird or that
such as

> *why don't you flap your wings*

and another time
to the one beside it

> *why don't you leap in the air*
> *and land again*

he laughed to himself when he realised
what he was doing
but persisted
for the fun of it

2010 (Part 2)

one day
he stamped his foot against the cold
just as he thought at the birds

    why don't you move away
    on the wire

when he glanced again at the flock
a space had appeared
and one of the birds had changed position

that night
he dreamed of a line of power —
almost transparent —
like a line of electricity —
running from his foot when it stamped

conveying his thought
to the bird

conversation and shock —
both —
to move the bird

the next evening
only two birds came
and when he stamped his foot toward them
they flew off immediately
and he nodded sagely to himself

truth is truth

power is truth

he did not know —
could not tell —
what causes birds to decide
where they will roost for the night
but he was certain that *this* flock
would not return again
to *that* winter wire

tune today

I wrote a tune today
that just came into my head

first I sang it
then I whistled
then I turned it into notes

it's not a song
just a tune I wrote today

it might have come from vienna
as a waltz upon the breeze

I might have picked it up in a signal
sent all the way from nashville

it could have been a reel
out of dublin

or the trailing voice of a harmonica
on the rising warm of a campfire

it might have come from anywhere
but it came to me
to whistle under my breath

I wrote it down
so I can share
and anytime you like
you can play it too

(anytime you like
but
play it on kazoo)

incomplete winter poem

the winter here
is beautiful

as the balmy autumn passes
and the trees let their leaves fall
to reveal the majesty
of branches raised skyward

a coolness creeps in
raising mist-wraiths and tendrils
on the stream
in early morning

the world
seems to pause for a moment
in the pre-dawn
between darkness and the light

a frozen stillness
broken by the solitary raucousness
of a kookaburra call
that reveals a landscape
blanched beneath thick frost

like a small blonde parcel
of dislocated tundra
still sleeping in the new light

a little (move)

she strides the stage
dressed in black
just a suggestion
in the darkness

> *move a little*
> *move a little*
> *one veil to the floor*

takes her time
no move too quickly
or she'll spoil the show

> *move a little*

she moves just a little

when she moves a little
more
another veil glides down
to the floor

counting the universal number by heart

the wobble of the earth
goes round and right around
eternity
in a slow time

from equinox to equinox
at one moment every year
it bobs its way
through star sign upon star sign
while almost twenty-six thousand
cycle away in multiples
of sixty

(*whisper*) four-thirty-two

sixty seconds
and sixty heartbeats add up
to one minute

and sixty minutes
comes twelve times
on the vernal day

forty-three thousand
two hundred separate heart pounds
each one
a *lub-de-da-da lub-de-dup*
that is just in time

I am counting the universe
around
and using just my heart
to measure god

when the man went inside

I was there on the day
that the man went inside

I tell you I was *there*
and I saw it all

he did nothing that I could tell
but to still the tides

when I looked into his eyes
there was only
a calm level sea
that went back for miles

I pulled out
before I could drown in it

he grew a smile on his lips
that was light —
like air —
and it lifted me
to see him smile that way

somehow it seemed
we both were flying for a while
until I shook my head and
almost
I fell over

when I had caught myself
steady once again
I looked across

and almost
I thought I saw him
but
a blink of my eye
and the shadow passed

2010 (Part 2)

the sun shone down like honey
where I thought of him
but
he was gone

and when I touched the place
where he had sat
my hand
was warm

un-bounded

he fell asleep in his armchair
in the lounge room
before the fire

chill winter began outside
on the doorstep
then rolled out in low-hung grey
as far as the trees and hills
that stood sentinel on the boundaries
in the distance

within his own four walls
he slept

.

.

.

when he opened his eyes
he seemed in darkness
but could see his hands
could see himself
without the aid of light

casting about he noticed
he was in *un*-winter
unwalled unchaired unclothed
he was a-*float*
that was a-*stand*
that was not *orientation*
or anything at all

curious
interesting

unhurried in the strange
he accustomed

2010 (Part 2)

until –
aware at last –
he scanned all points around him
and could not locate
the trees

he missed the hills

no clouds no sky
no colour
no line of the horizon
he could not find a beginning
nor an end

he could find
no thing

the trembling
when it began
was centred in his belly
and rose to touch a smear of bile
upon his lips
before he opened his mouth wide –
without thinking –
and began to scream

dream land

and I wept at the beauty
of the land I saw

the earth
on which I stood

where my tear fell
a tree grew
both high and wide
in a blinking of my eye
it was there

I bent low before the mighty
bowed down my head
until I had touched the ground
and knew
it was good

the hunter

I am the hunter
I creep near
to my prey

I leap
grab and tumble
to subdue

then I get nervous

then I get weird

> *what if the prey is the pursuer*
>
> *what if all I entrap*
> *is myself*
>
> *what if I grow lost in the netting*
> *never to be free again*
>
> *the cords growing tighter*
>
> *how can I know*
> *that I've caught the right creature*
>
> *what if my spear*
> *pierces my own eye*
>
> *how will I see what stands*
> *right there before me*

I am the hunter
I steal after spoor
and run over pathways
that only appear in my mind

I creep near to my prey
and although I am hungry
I cannot lay my hand
on the beast

I smile
as it runs from me

shake my head and turn
towards home

an aspara-guy song

a lone asparagus lifted his head
he'd been lying low
for the winter

I was just passing
not near but enough
to intercept on the wind
what he said

> hello oh my sweet peas
> my tomatoes and pumpkins
> hello
> are you waking
> my carrot-topped friends
>
> where have you gone
> are you underground
> sleeping
> it is time my dears
> to ascend
>
> shuck off the dullness
> that lying in frost brings
> the humming of bees says
> the chill is at end
>
> so put on your green clothes
> and dance in the springtime
>
> yes
> put on your green things
> and dance

diving in the petrified sea

the doctors donned their diving bells
and stethoscopes

> *probed the wreck*

> *finger-tapped for echoes*

they fossicked
through the slurried dregs
of his old battlefield
found nothing
but an absence of sounds
deep down
in the hard-lung forest
of no-man's air

while we watched the old man
drowning
one shallow breath
at a time

the return

when the prodigal claimed a seat
at the bedside
the old man cried

    you see

he called

    do you see
    there is love left in the world
    and my life
    has not been wasted

hh jesus

and jesus is gone
hip hooray
I'm not buying anything
door to door
today

shout out the tidings
no need to stay hiding
for jesus is gone
so they say

and I'm singing
from my door to yours
hip hooray

since I stopped

since I have stopped writing well
this pen is a gn tool
an artifact
familiar only in its shape
useful for a certain utility
in creating a line of numerals
a list of chores

since I stopped writing so well
as once I did
(in my pomp)
this paper represents a geometric shape
filled with hungry lines
that devour embryonic thoughts
almost before I can think them
and turn stories into undifferentiated swirls
of blue-black ink
that I have no wish to unravel

it is hot outside my window
the season has begun to burn
while I hide in the shaded darkness
lying on my bed
eyes closed
seeking refuge within a restless dream

the air is bracing itself
to be a long dry summer

since I stopped writing my joy every day
I find myself speaking too often
too loudly
but none of the words are worth saving

nothing for my pen
to mark on the paper

nothing for the lines —
those empty lines —
to keep

a glorious whirly and home-roast beans

I have bought the popcorn-maker whirligig
and wait now
for a candy thermometer to install
on the side of the lid

it has a winding device in the handle
to push two twirling blades around

and today I received my green beans
in the mail

four little bags
air tight
from Ethiopia and Brazil
and from Peru

they hardly look like coffee
there is no aromatic smell
and they are small
almost innocuous
as though they could not hold
all that I've been promised

but I'll try

green beans in a popcorn maker
twirled around upon the stove

that's coffee-making
and I can't wait to hear
the first *crack-crack*

the second *crack*
and *crack*
of browning beans

and aroma
drifting down the street
calling the neighbours to their doors
to sniff

2010 (Part 2)

what's that . . .

what's that

the coffee man of john street
is roasting beans
right there on his stove-top

oh

what a glorious day

Frank Prem

for the (rockfall) record

*all right fella's
so the sky fell in
and here we are
a hundred miles down
underground*

*let's assess the situation
objectively
there's less of us to pull up
than they had in Chile*

*but we're trapped deeper
and it might take longer*

*everything depends on how they weigh
the waiting*

*we're a hundred yards lower
so if we allow
maybe two days more
to cater for sickness and infirmity
I think we've got a show*

*when they reach us —
eventually —
with a telephone
we'll ask the officials to attend
our attempt in The Guinness Book
of Cave-In Records*

*we'll set a world mark
and get a book deal
while we're waiting*

who's got a quirky story . . .

does anyone have a famous friend . . .

what brought you to the coal mines in the first place

was it for the romance . . .

2010 (Part 2)

what do you dream of in the dark

*let's ask for media coaching
while the dragging hours pass*

*in the meantime just keep waiting
listen for a sound
that isn't rock-falls raining
always closer*

*my friends
are you still here with me . . .*

*somebody needs to speak
because all alone
and all enclosed by darkness
is like a kind of madness*

*let's hold on for the record
one more hour   another day
surely someone's coming down
to find us*

*hello boys
say hello to me*

hello boys

hello

hello

Whirley-gigging the coffee

I've always been a drinker of pretty scungy coffee. As a young man, I first became accustomed to drinking a powdery institution blend that we jokingly called '*the sweepings off the floor*'. It was warm and it was wet and it was free, and I didn't know much better at the time, so that was that. To this day in my working life I will carry a polystyrene cup filled with '*sweepings*' around with me without complaint.

My taste in coffee for consumption at home has always been marginally more sophisticated that that of the work situation. In the confines of my personal coffee palace, I graduated up the café chain to drinking a solution of granules, preferably of a dark colour. Classy, that!

And when out, café latte at the conclusion of lunch, perhaps a cappuccino or a flat white . . . de rigueur on all outings of a social nature.

But then, nearly seven years ago, things began to change. The lady in my life had a touch of the fanatic about her pursuit of the finer things in life, and introduced me to the pleasures of the stove-top brew, and coffee began to assume a weighty depth that involved the senses — taste and aroma — to be sure, but overridingly took on the qualities of a deep ritual that held a spiritual undertone.

Beans by the kilo bag. Dark roasted for espresso. Eight teaspoons of beans into the grinder we rescued from my grandmother's house after she died. The heaven-scented coarse grind that resulted spooned into a stove-top coffee maker for steam to be forced through the ground beans then reconstituted by a mesmeric bubbling, hissing, boiling process into the rich brown liquid that filled our kitchen with that unmistakable aroma.

Topped with boiled full-cream milk. Ah, *joy!*

This journey involved harnessing the mundane in support of the miraculous. Where, for example, could I find a replacement rubber seal for the hardened, mangy one we'd had since time began, or a new sieve basket for a stove-top coffee machine? We replaced two machines before we found our answer on the internet. For a fellow who started out happy to make do with powdered dregs, the journey towards coffee-snobbishness has been a rapid one. In no time at all, supermarket roast beans have attracted a dubious suspicion. How good are they? How long since they were roasted? Where did they come from? Are they really Arabica, or is the label fudging the truth? And are they ethical?

Again, the internet acted as a great enabler. For a modest bid-price, freshly roasted beans, from the chosen country of origin are now delivered to our door. Ahh, just taste the difference! How good are we?!

And how satisfying this ritual has become.

But, still, there is further to travel on this journey. We're interested in trying to become independent of processed food and excessive packaging as much as possible. We enjoy resurrecting and preserving old traditions and incorporating them into our daily lives, and there's another step back into the past involving coffee making that teases us both, on the periphery of being do-able . . . and that's the creation of coffee from a handful of green beans by roasting them ourselves, complete with a roasting dary and of course, the requisite blog and photos. Seriously tempting . . . but how?

My research turned up a marvelous little beginners guide to the world of coffee and home roasting titled *Home Coffee Roasting – Romance and Revival by Kenneth Davids (St Martins Griffin, New York, 1996)*. It's a wonderful introduction to the rich history and development of the coffee trade, regions, types and styles, and specifically instructs on the requirements and processes involved in roasting coffee at home.

Only halfway through the book and I was eagerly saddling up for this new journey. I wanted the romance that it described, where the old men and women in Italian villages sat out on their balconies twice a week to roast a couple of days worth of coffee at a time. I wanted the civility of the coffee ceremony where respect was shown by the trouble taken to prepare the coffee with the guest in attendance, as witness. I wanted to become the master of a simple art that no-one in my circle of acquaintance has imagined, let alone performed.

Some of the equipment seemed a little preposterous. Whereas the pictures in the book were of various stove-top and barrel style coffee bean roasters, what my little book recommended was a pop-corn maker with a crank handle. Something that I've never encountered in Australia, let alone in common use. Nonetheless, a *'Whirley'* stove-top pop-corn maker was soon ordered, all the way from America. (My whims know no geographic boundaries). Also, a candy thermometer, and a two kilogram starter batch of green beans from each of four distinct coffee regions of the world.

Total cost of this initial equipment (including the book that served as my bible) has come to $A98.14. A bargain at the price, in my opinion.

This morning the final stages of the adventure took place. As soon as the thermometer arrived, we drilled a hole in the top of the Whirley-gig to house it in and began the process. The basic steps are as follows:

Heat the Whirley to around 230 degrees Centigrade.

Pour in the beans (we used 100gm of Ethiopian Gambella Sundried beans for the first batch).

Stir the beans steadily throughout (doesn't have to be non-stop, but has to be constant to get an even roast).

Watch for smoke to rise, listen for the beans to *'crack'*. This step took no more than two minutes to be reached.

Start taking peeks at the beans every thirty seconds to a minute to check their colour. What we were aiming for initially was a colour that matched or was a little lighter than the beans we had previously bought for our morning brew.

Take the beans off the heat when the colour is a tiny bit lighter than what you want to achieve. This is because the beans will keep roasting for awhile from accumulated heat.

Rapidly cool the beans by passing from colander to colander to let air get at them. This is best done outside as there is a husk still attached to the green beans that separates during the roast and this will blow away with a gentle breeze.

Ten minutes after beginning, the roast was ready to come off the stove.

What we found we were left with was a deeply rich brown bean that was significantly oily on the surface. The colour was slightly darker than we were aiming for, but just looked gorgeous, conjuring archetypal images of a sun-drenched Africa. The beans lost about twenty-five percent of their weight during the roast, due to the green beans being loaded up with moisture. Much of the smoke that is produced during the roast is this moisture evaporating from the bean. The roasted beans are also significantly larger than the green beans due to expansion.

The experts suggest that beans are at their best for drinking between four and perhaps twenty-four hours after the roasting. They slowly but relentlessly lose aspects of their flavour from that point on as oxygen starts to have a deteriorating effect on the beans.

There was no way, however, that we were going to wait for hours or days before trying out what we'd created. We were up for a grind immediately. What we found was a coffee that is rich in aroma, though not as overpowering as I'd been half-expecting. The taste was more bitter on the tongue than we were accustomed to but a nice strong brew to drink. There is a lingering tingle of coffee aftertaste in my mouth as I write, some hours after the cup was consumed.

Tomorrow, we'll sample the roast after twenty-four hours of ageing to compare. In another two days, we'll roast a second batch, perhaps aiming for a lighter coloured bean. Three days after that, we may try a different region of the world. We have definitely begun an exciting new journey into the romantic revival of home coffee bean roasting!

giggling the ivories

it's a long time since I reached
to touch the ivory
I never have played well
in fact you'd hardly say
that I could play
at all

but for a time I sat
with my thumb on *middle c*
as a place to begin
and then on better days
I might sound something out
just like a tune

now
the piano sits behind me
waiting patiently
while I avoid the subject
of my playing

there'll be a better hour
and a better time one day
and I won't feel
the *clumsy-creature* blues

I will do the repetitions
practice as I can and
when I should
until the ivories giggle
like a girl amused
and the scales step nimbly
from fulsome tone to semi steps

in *c*
and in *d*
major minor in the sharpest key

when I reach out
again
to the piano

only a four

I've got a good one for you Frank:

> *Why did the tennis player go up and down the river?*
>
> *Because he was Pat Rafter.*

What would you give that one, Frank,
an eight?

Only a four!
You must be a hard marker, Frank.

What about this one, then . . .

2011

a letter to the royal society

dear sirs
I wish to report a discovery

I have found the land again

it lies within a brown loam
that crumbles beneath my feet

with the hoe
I can form it into a furrow
or raise up a hill

into the new valley I have placed a potato
and from the hill
I am able to fashion a bed of planted things

yes
I have found the land again

look
it fills the lines on the palm
of my hands
and lies under the nails

sirs
do you see here
this wonderful thing
I have new-found

chin-chin christmas

christmas biscuits
and dry cheese crackers

champagne in the middle
of the day

strong coffee
brewed right after the grinder

it is a christmas for two
in our home on the hill

the trees whisper carols
at each movement of the wind

clouds hurry by
to be raining some elsewhere
while *we*
are at christmas

good luck
and chin-chin

2011

with a view to the sweet-grass

the walk up the track
into the forest
is a meditation of butterflies
and the unpredictable scent
of eucalyptus rising

monarchs reign here
individuals in hundreds
courting sets of five and six
twirl in a meandering pursuit
of some would-be queen

> *a paddock of rolled hay*
>
> *the scrub-wood valley*
>
> *the rise of plantation conifers*
> *thirty years dense*
>
> *full green*

here
on the rise that is the end
of the walk
lushest grasses grow

four tender stalks . . . five
to be carried back down the hill
then shredded
into dinner for the faithful one
who sniffs the view
at her mistress's feet
each evening

feeling the arrival

I've got myself a brand new set
of scratches
from down in the garden

it seems like
even on a day like this
in the heat
I can't make myself stop
and I'm drawn down into our jungle
with the secateurs
and my bow-saw

you were no sooner
out of the door and on your way
than I found myself speculating

what would I do with so much
of my own idle time
on my hands

and like an itch
the garden called
for there is dead wood on the boundary
to be sawed
and room enough left
to expand the vegetables
in raised beds
or just
by grubbing around
with a mattock or a hoe
raking smooth the final outcome

I think we came up here
to plant seed
then to watch ourselves grow

2011

to dance in the night
beneath the shadow of the sky
so dark
we can't see where to place
our steps

the birds call
a song about home
and when I listen to them
I feel my own arrival

and when I look at you
on your return
I can feel this
as *our* home

everyday changing

every day I'm growing simpler

I guess that getting older
has a price

I can't move so fast
and I can't hold everything
that's swirling around me

but I'm ok

being a simple man
doesn't mean that I've turned stupid

it doesn't mean I'm losing control
or winding down

it just means my heart comes alive
to the sound of birdsong

it means I feel hope right in my hand
when I hold the loam
out of my garden

every day I hold that hand up
to slow the world down
just a little

it's not that I can't follow
or comprehend events
that swirl around me

but I don't want them

I have enough

it doesn't mean dementia
it doesn't mean I have no place
or anyone to talk to

it just means I know who I am
and that's sufficient

2011

it means one best friend I can touch
is everything I own
and ever want to

every day I'm growing simpler
but not *less*

when I hold my hand up
I can touch you
and every day
I find that's enough

not listening to a flood

I am not listening
to the stories about floods

they are an inundation

on every tv channel
I have seen waters overflowing

tears being wept like rivers

speechless people
telling incoherent stories
of how
they have never seen the like before
who thought the first time
three weeks ago
was their disaster
but here it is *again*
running in through open doorways
dismissing out of hand
restraining walls

in the city
bargain basement shopping
has to relocate
by several floors

bring your credit in a boat

but I'm not watching
I'm not listening
over and over again
throughout the day

it fascinates me

mesmerizing
like a python
eye to eye
or
a glimpse into oblivion

2011

it's just the tv
turned on for background company
but the premier
is weeping
for a life once took for granted

swept away
on rising waters
while a commentator I am ignoring
speaks of economic recovery

there is state to be rebuilt
and infrastructure —
it seems —
will save us all

a quick latte (a long black)

my coffee grows on a hill somewhere
around Kandara
in Kenya

my coffee ripens beneath the sun out there
in Rutsiro
or Rubavu
in Rwanda

my coffee is stored in the monsoon air
of the Malabar coast
in India

    enjoy your latte

my coffee dries where a slow breeze whiles
on Pico Turquino
in Cuba

my coffee is named for the exotic style
of San Isidro
in Costa Rica

my coffee arrives in green bean piles
from La Bendicion
in Nicaragua

    sip your black

your coffee awaits you, served with a smile
from out of my garage
where I roast it brown

so

    enjoy your latte

    sip your black

2011

soar around the world
with the cup to your lips
fly high fly high
then
come on back

sip your latte

the a-philosopher

he believed in anti-science
de-volution
ir-relativity

uncommon sense
outer ears
un-numbered eyes
and the unstoppable rise
of a-gravity

but most of all he believed
in the universe
un-expanding

growing smaller
all the time

2011

about thunder and lightning

how many times must I tell you
don't play with thunder
he's likely to lose his temper

dark moods become him
black clouds surround
and if you won't take advice
don't come crying

thunder doesn't like to be
messed about

~

how many times must I tell you
don't mess with lightning
lightning won't look but you
will burn

he's flash and he's fast

you'll look black
when you're fried
and lightning won't care
if you're even there

~

how many times must I tell you
do your playing in the rain
the rain is true
as an arrow

so lightly it falls
from the sky
to your clothes
and you might be wet as a puddle

but
the rain will stand you
straight up and tall

if you must play with weather
go play
with the rain

dirty walk

let's go for a walk
among the trees down the back
the dog needs to go
and there's a eucalypt
that's just in flower

taste that blackberry

look at our swamp
after the rain

if we cleared these ferns away
I could make this a parkland

by the way
the apples are coming on well
nearly ripe
and the plums have shown purple

wander home
by the vegetables
take some time
to pull weeds and thin carrots
whisper nothings
to encourage the beans skywards

yellow squash are rampant

baby broccoli are showing off
number one haircuts
and a promise that they'll turn out well

when we go for a walk
because the dog has to go
among the trees down the back
I wear gumboots

I wear gardening clothes

and I come home dirty

cry green

sometimes my nakedness
shames me
and I wish I had brought
some barrier
a concealment
to place between myself
and the searchlight you apply
that exposes me
nook and cranny
like a desert landscape
holding nothing but its own dust
as a cloud that obscures
in arid bitterness
a crying out for green

my place in nothing

and how could I not worship
when I turn my face
towards the sky

there are stars there
designed to overfill my head
with an idea of what small is
and my place
within the scheme

and I know I am nothing

but who else is there
to gaze
wide open to the colours within black
and to the pinpoint indicators
of a place where mightiness once shone
and see the scheme

and I know I am everything

all of it is for me
and it is nothing

cruising the cat

if you bounce on the tiller
of your tail
you will lose all control
over where we might sail

but if we stroke your fur smooth
we could strike the right groove
then spread paws to fly
from the rail

an air holder

walter wise went walking
through the gloom

    (ta ta tum)

to clean the path he swept it
with a broom

    (ta ta tum)

with the sun in his eyes *(ta-ta ta tum)*
he thought it quite nice *(ta-ta ta tum)*
so walter hummed to himself
this tune

    (ta ta tum)

pitter-patter

there's a light pitter-patter
of the rain coming down
it's not down-pouring
hardly even falling
more just floating to the ground

I can hear it on my tin-roof
I can see it through the glass
there is a light pitter-patter
as the rains dances past

my career in solitaire

my first mistake
was over-playing to the aces

the second was using a heart
as main suit

the third time was going back
to where I'd already been

the fourth thing I got wrong
was my own blindness

and the last that I recall
was trying again

things they don't describe too well (at all)

they don't really tell you
that you'll make a dead man vomit
they just say

    keep the airway clear

they don't tell you that
the kiss of life is a test
of resolution over disgust

they don't describe the change
in his temperature
from warm to cool
to colder

and they don't describe the sound
of the gurgling
every time you give a breath
every time you pump his heart
every time you expect that he might cough
and start to wake up

and they don't describe the moment
when your doubt becomes conviction
but you keep on pushing
and you keep on breathing
and you keep on doing it anyhow

just the way they told you

there's surely a lot that they don't tell you
and you have to hold on
to the hope
that there'll be someone close enough
to say
when you can stop

2011

hush Stanley town

it's quiet here today
in Stanley
where we moved to get away
from traffic
and the sound of a big town's noise

it's a shock to find that
even in the hills
there's no escape
no way to find the peace of meditation
of thinking about life
from far away

a small disappointment
that we put over
to one side
and weigh against the good life
that we've found

but today is not like that
because it's quiet here

no sound of roosters
there's no magpies
no cockies and no wrens today

and I can't hear so much as a peep
from the neighbours dogs

their car went out this morning
and there's been silence ever since
except for the rustle of a breeze
exploring fuji apples

the water pumps are still
and there's no chain-saw sounding anywhere
the rhythmic double-pound
of shotguns among the chestnut trees
has been silenced

perhaps the harvest is over
or the cockatoos have gone
or perhaps there's been a vote passed
in parliament to decree

a welcome quiet over Stanley
today

dog bats (for the best spot)

I'm lying down with the pooch

she got the best spot
in front of the fire
where I'm nuzzling in
while she bats at me
with a potentially lethal paw
but I don't believe her
when she growls

I can growl too
and I've got my own paw
to bat back at her
and we're both flailing growls
and ducking under smiting blows
and smiling at each other
in front of the heater

the pooch is lying down ear the hearth
she's fought off my challenge
and remains queen
of the hearth spot
that catches all the best warmth
from the fire

and I'm still growling
over by the coffee table
while licking at my wounds
after a comprehensive beating
but don't really mean it

I'll bat her better
next time

rooster morning

a rooster calls (*koo-koo-ka-roo*)
at the first sign the dawn brings
he's got to sing the fowl-yard
on it's way

when the hens arise (*ka-koo-re-ooo*)
all soft down and clucking
he can tilt his crown
then strut all day

koo-koo-ka-roo
it's a rooster morning
wake the day
with a clarion call

ka-koo-re-ooo
rooster dawning
here's a song
for your hens to lay

weighing nothing

I weighed my self on a feather
I did fly
away with the first chill wheeze
of the morning

flew for a while
then walked another mile
light as the sun
at first yawning

let me help you stand
oh brother take my hand
the movement of this air
seems absurd

but when you weigh your heart
upon the feather of the sky
you best allow for the action
of the bird

Frank Prem

the moon concedes in three parts

call the sun
I wish to parley

tell him that I seek to talk

I will cede to him the day
that he may bright and burn it
while I skulk
in the darkness of the night
as a vanquished satellite should do

but
I will light the sky as well
for though beaten now
yet I was as mighty once
and still I can use light
yes still
I will keep a tiny something from him
that hardly he will miss

so call the sun
make pax between us
I will only claim the sky
when he has turned his head

and once a cycle I will hide myself
to meditate on my defeat

but once in that cycle I will glow
brighter than the brightest stars
to remember who and what I was

then
once in every turning
I will enter –
humbled –
into his light
pale and weak yet I'll be there
to show that honour lies
within obeisance

as flowers strewn

I am strewing flowers
for fallen soldiers

attending solemn services
in my finery and nervousness
for deaths that seem so purposeless
with all these miles between

far away they strike the ground
in some desert and mountain hell
a tolling of the bell is meant
to call their spirits home
back from where they fell
now breathless
our armed and camouflaged emissaries
of nought but good intent
and in some way to atone

by strewing de-petaled flowers
for fallen soldiers
in the colours of a long long way
such a very long
long way away
from home

The way in which Barbara can be likened to a particular kind of goat.

Ah now, that's Barbara. Barbara is a bit of a story.

You see, we've all been raised on the stories about Alpaca's as flock guardians, but they have their limitations. If the dog pack has a bit of kelpie, or collie in their blood, they'll keep circling and rounding the mob for hours. The alpacas charge at them and are very protective, just like the stories tell, but after a while they seem to wilt.

It's as though they get a sense that the task is futile. Beyond them.

Then they'll turn tail and run off to hide.

That's the point where you'll lose twenty ewes in a night. They'll have tried hard, but the wild dog packs we get through here are too big an ask.

Anyway, I was reading an article about how they use donkeys over in America to keep the coyotes away, and I thought it might be worth a try. Hence Barbara.

She was a run-of-the-mill free-to-a-good-home donkey and in her own right has been no trouble. She's taken to the sheep and the alpacas and they all happily co-inhabit the paddock. The thing that's happened though is that stock loss to dogs has dropped to near nothing.

Barbara isn't like the alpacas. She won't quit when the packs come around.

You ought to see her – ears back, braying like a banshee and going at them with teeth and hooves – again and again.

Formidable.

2011

You'd think that saving the sheep from dogs would be enough, but Barbara has another trick.

Moving the mob from paddock to paddock, or into the pens for moving to the abattoir used to be quite tricky, but works like a charm now. I just come to the fence here, by the gate, and bang on it with an iron rod. Barbara pops her head up, as though to sniff the breeze to figure out what's happening, then lets out a huge, long bray.

She starts trotting over towards me and all the mob line up behind, following in her hoof prints, all the way into the next paddock, or onto the transport, if that's where we want them. Never a second bleat.

She seems to take pride in being an honorary farmhand, and for me, it's a positive pleasure to have her aboard.

hard words

and I find as I age
that the words come harder

>   *where is the silver-tongued voice*
>   *of my youth*

perhaps there's a time when everything
seems new
perhaps there's a time
when you've seen too much

and how many ways
can you write down everything you know
I listen to myself
when I'm speaking
and I think I know all the things
that I am going to say
before I say them

every argument
is too familiar
every thrill was lived *way back*
in *once upon a time*
and the pen in my hand
is the only thing
that feels just a little too near
to almost unfamiliar

until the loops emerge
the words all join
and I can breathe again
at last

it seems there's still something
I haven't said
some new thing that I've just now seen
and another way to tell a story
that I've told many times before

2011

I find as I age
the words come
just a little bit harder

a short statement from the latest arrival

*I wish to make a statement
the latest new-arrival said
I wish to tell you all
about my life*

when I was born . . .

was the way he began
in a slow-build that took no account
of time

but as I trod lightly
between the stones
and the mounds in the grass
the sound I heard was the
woo woo woo
of the wind

kook-ing apples

kooka-by
kooka-by you laugh-er
sitting down low
on my apple tree

kooka-fly
kooka-fly your supper
is waiting down below my
red-apple tree

kookaburra tell me
when dawn's set to come
and kookaburra tell me
when this day's work is done

kooka-by
kooka-by I'm laughing
at you perching so low
on my apple tree

2012 (Part 1)

2012 (Part 1)

all in a day

constructing
a saw-stool
followed olives

brining
the olives
was after the path

bricking
a pathway
trailed the irrigation

laying
a pipe-line
was right after breakfast

pass me the coffee
please
I'm not sure I'm awake

hot koala

a koala snorted
from the trees across the road
calling his lover to play
I thought to myself
she must be hard up
or there's something in his call
that doesn't translate
because it sounded like a bear
with his toe caught in a grate
and I hoped that he was better
when they met face-to-face
and I hoped that he was more
in every way

a koala snorted
from a tree across the road
called out in the middle of the day
I thought to myself
well he must be hard up
for there was something in his call
that was a little heart-breaking
sounded like he couldn't bear
another night of waiting
and I hoped he'd find a mate
who'd be cuddly face to face
and I hoped that every snort
would be repaid

have you ever heard a koala
call out in the night
it's like a sore head
in a bar-room
itching for a fight
and he gives it everything
that he's got
must be the eucalyptus leaves
that make him so hot

2012 (Part 1)

s-s-s-s-strength

the visitor on the verandah
with a sinuous slip was away

>	*into*
>	*out of*

the basket of washing

head down towards the uncut grass
sliding *ess-es ess-es*
hell for leather

one blink and it was gone

well before my legs would move

before I could cry aloud

>	*a s-s-s-s . . .*
>	*honey*
>	*it's a s-s-s. . .*

I call my self a strong man
strong enough to meet my burdens
but the other day
I saw a copperhead on the verandah
yet when I looked again
it wasn't there

just a ripple in the gentled grass
and already just a memory
that made me jumping-tense

>	*when the dog sniffs*
>	*at a sheet of tin*

>	*when the wind kisses*
>	*a stray tickle of my hair*

every time I think
of the sinuous sliding
ess-ess-ess of snake

I'm not really very strong . . .

not very strong
at all

to a tree

blossoms and bees
and butterflies
are bowing the red-flower gum
down to where I am

towards the ground

the humming stops for a moment
as I place my face near
then surrounds me
until I'm one with
the tree

and the song is of liquid gold
in the sunshine . . .

the breeze . . .

is fluttered wings
that kiss my cheek
with nectar sweet
as warm honey

the blossoms and the bees
and the butterflies
and me
are bowing
together with the red gum
to the ground

it's a kind of worship
it's a kind of gift
it's a kind of heaven
in the sunshine of today

buccaneers

avast my hearty
better shiver your what's-it
the buccaneering bower birds have come

show us your apple trees

yo-ho a party
has come down a-raider-ing
so beat the autumn bower bird drum

take me to your vegetables

they are hungry
they are twenty
they are voracious
they are forty
they are insatiable
they're one hundred

bower birds have come
to raid your garden
and every bit of green is gold

was that a seedling

hop hop stand
then swash-a-bit and buckle
the bower birds have come

ha ha my little cabbage

a crimson in the apples (crimson rosella: platycercus elegans)

I supervised the apples
through the summer
watched them redden up and ripen
beneath the sun

covered them with nets
and peered between the small square mesh
to see —

> *were they whole*
>
> *were they misshapen*
>
> *were they eaten*

and when the nights began to cool
I commenced the harvest

only the best fruit for the larder

anything with blemishes
or peck marks
for bottling
or for sauce

> *fuji*
> *five crown*
> *johnathon's*
>
> *royal gala*

and as each tree was done
I left some of the ripest
to celebrate the autumn

> *your gift*

and I see you this morning
climbing through the five crown tree

mister crimson rosella
what remains there
is all yours

sing about your pleasure

feel free

invite your mates

at the end of harvest season
in the golden cool
of a brightened autumn day
I bid you
fine pickings
and good winter

2012 (Part 1)

world tour

I shall now proceed to take
the very best verse
from my greatest poem
on a world-wide tour
of beechworth
including wooragee

three special shows
in the empty old hall
just off the wodonga road
at leneva

there'll be one in the hut
usually set aside
for the scouts and girl guides
on second street
in yackandandah

I will wow the crowd
beside the quick-fill dam
at osborne's flat
when I turn round
with my entourage
to recommence the tour
by going back again

never forgetting —
no I'll not overlook —
the sell outs

because
there are no tickets available
for markwood or everton

and there's nothing at all in whorouly
where the floods also toured
this summer

I think they'll like me
tremendously
when I call in
by-the-way
at tarrawingee

so thank you

thank you el dorado

thank you
murmungee

it means such a lot to hear the echo
of your heartfelt applause
around mount pilot

you have been the best
the very best
of my audience

2012 (Part 1)

reflection at the start (of a croissant)

it's a day
like any other
in the tourist town

the bakery is open around dawn
and I'm lined up
with a newspaper under my arms
to get a coffee

twenty minutes quiet
before I drag myself to work

because a rostered shift
takes no account
of Sundays
or Public Holidays
and one set of hours is much the same
as the next

but today the girl behind the counter
sidles alongside me
to slip a small brown bag
of toasted cheese inside a croissant
onto my table

> *here you go*
> *this one's on the house*
>
> *if we don't look out for each other*
> *on a day like this*
> *nobody else will*

so while it's quiet
before the crowds roll in
take a moment for some breakfast
and contemplation

before the chaos
that will be this holiday
take just a moment
for reflection

happy easter

2012 (Part 1)

the loquat flower:the frost:the winter

the loquat tree is flowering white
on the first frost day
of autumn

I object to this fact on principle
I object to the chill
so soon after a poor excuse
for summer
that held hardly any real heat
and barely any sun
far too much of rain
and was here
far too briefly

I'm bracing now
for all-day fires and a rug
to keep my knees warm

any old day now
I'm sure it will snow

and the fog will descend
to conceal the town
that I usually see
from on my hill top

the loquat's in flower
the frost is on the grass
and I'm already cold

as cold
as if
it was winter

the love poem for you

this is the love poem
I write for you
every time you leave

in the freedom
of a lonely room
an empty house
I take the pen up again
for you

this time I thought
I would have no words
to say

nothing I could share

but your absence led —
drew me —
through the endless hours
the desolation of the dog
and the fire lit
for me alone
to write this poem

this poem again

a few words
in your absence
to mark my love for you

a liquidautumn poem

the liquidambar tree
is turning burgundy

I drink it with my eyes

press a leaf
between these pages

call it poetry

liquidambar poetry

painting the liquid amber — an autumn day in May

take a palette
pink and mauve
five pointed leaves
on yellow

crimson onto green

leaves are falling
thick like snow
in shaded rainbow hues

shoosh shoosh
colours whisper
rustle
as I move my feet

the artist's work
has fallen
to embrace me

scarlet robin on guard duty

first
the fleet of yellow-tails
are a ripple in the carpet
of paddock grass

then
the thornbills in the trees
who are never far
from their cousins

>*busy busy*
>*leap and peck*
>*clean the wood of tucker*

>*busy busy*
>*scour the grass*
>*clear the ground of tucker*

and there he is
on the fence this time

there he is
on the fallen gate

there he is
with his star ablaze
guardian of his flock-mates

always there
when the troop arrives
always checking the vista

always red
and black and white
always
in safety to keep them

warmer on the verandah

the scrub-wren
is hopping on the verandah
it's too wet and cold
out on the lawn

the grass is in-between
hard frost
and soft snow

underneath the wood-box
is warmer
don't you know

the scrub-wren
is hopping on the verandah
and waiting for the winter
to blow

winter numb

these are the boring days
of winter

not even trees
can hold their leaves
after so many days of frost
and rain

the air is full of bite
for there is snow
just above me
on the hills

and hail
is falling in my head

my brain
is numb

2012 (Part 2)

like rain

there's been no rain
for weeks and now
I'm watering

clouds are threatening
with a spit or two
and
they say there might be storms

temperature's dropped
and a front is blowing through
but
it's just a drop

is not enough

I'm still moving a sprinkler around
and thinking

> *come on*
> *come on*

I'll stop using the hose
when the water falls
like rain

dry drowning

humidity is high
I
am close to drowning
in my sweat

there is no breeze
there is no air
no need to hold my nose
as I go under

and again a day

hours slide like water
through my fingers

pour the morning
spill the noon
empty the evening

another cup . . .

start again
the day

solo

strum strum strum
strum
strum strum strum

solo

strum-a-strum

best apple

the best apple
in the world
was a gala

it came from our orchard

it spoke
just once
said

    crunch

good cake

blood plums
for *good cake*

straight from tree . . .

to bake-dish . . .

to oven

the smell
pursues me
room to room

the woodshed has a floor

you laid it

laid it twice

It looks perfect

> *watertight*
> *level*
> *sound and solid*

ready for winter wood

certain people

. . . are a bitch

certain lives
should not be sustained

there is far too much
ugliness
in *certain* people

trios

three king parrots
on the guttering
studying my moves

three kookaburras
in the tree
above where I am working

three times
the wrens
have surrounded me

in three days
I have been *birded*
thrice

work benign

honey bees
on the fennel flowers

wrens among the canes
of raspberry

fantails dance
in the air
above us

we are all working
beneath a gentle sun

a benign sky

warm weather

I got up this morning
the weather was

>   *light falling through the trees*
>   *dapple dapple dapple*

I went out this morning
the weather was

>   *light spilling on the ground*
>   *yellow golden yellow*

I got up this morning
the weather was

>   *light kissing warm my face*
>   *dapple golden yellow*

>   *warm*

health gone

what a day was yesterday

I failed to find my health
maybe I dropped it
down
behind my armchair

and so the flu came
the cough came
the rasping throat

the nose ran
and my eyes shed tears

where is my health gone

man flu

aching bones
keep me alive

it's just too painful
to die
right now

water level

water level

>*thunk thunk*

>*boom boom*

>*thunk thunk*

>*boom boom*

autumn is here
with the tank
half empty

a garden page

tomato potato beetroot
parsnip fennel carrot
white radish aubergine capsicum
chili broccoli cabbage cauliflower
turnip swede brussels sprout
blueberry raspberry strawberry
black current gooseberry jostaberry
blackberry cucumber snap peas
sugar peas purple bean green bean
borlotti fava bean runner bean
bush bean brown onion green onion
shallot potato onion tree onion garlic
leek coriander oregano rocket celery
celeriac silverbeet mushrooms
walnut pecan macadamia hazelnut
almond apple pear rhubarb radish

term end

and the sound
fills the hall

voices rising in harmony

out to one side
we strum our ukes
as if lives
depend upon it

wren-cen-tralia

a seething of wrens
catchies the corner
of my eye
every direction I turn

the garden is alive
with feathered cherubim

living lightly

my tale of mushrooms
on old newspaper
grown in the garden shed
was published today
in a new newspaper
destined
for the garden shed
and mushrooms

old dogs

we're tired dogs
we seem to want
to go to bed together

at the exact same time

I hit the mattress —
in the middle of the bed —
and say

    aaah

she doesn't say a thing
but flops down on a blanket
in the corner

just a tired dog

we are tired old dogs
and around about our bedtime
she gets snappy

while I can't think
of anything more
to say

except to tell her

    good night
    you tired old dog

we're a couple
of tired old dogs

storm alone

I'm listening for the sound of rain
borne down on the wind
that circles around the storm

I'm listening for the swinging of the trees
fluffing their branches
beneath the falling weather

but all I hear is my own
ragged breath
winding through the obstacles
that are my sinuses
and the scratch of a pencil
across this paper

I
am the only soul
that can be heard

when did a storm
become so lonely

Joseph Cambell - Mythology

Joseph Cambell - Mythology

the first lord's song

the king is dead
I know
for it fell to me to kill him

with my noose
I strangled
until he was gone

I wished him only good
I bore no malice

but when the stars align —
their circuit complete —
each must play his part
and so . . .

done is done

long live the king
hail his rise
how alive he seems
with so much to do
under the sun

and at night the stars
already trekking away

I watch each day his deeds
rejoicing

we watch each night —
my noose and I —
the stars

for the time that yet must come
when they align once again

I am first lord
to the king

a knowledge of the red

and he will come to me now —
already I anticipate it —
to tell me what he knows of red coals

as though I am an ignorant
who has never taken time
never looked
inside my mind

>   *I have watched the glow*
>   *when the fire dimmed*
>   *I have seen the red and black*
>   *and gazed into embers*
>   *that grow brighter then retract*
>   *like a tide*
>
>   *the flow of colour motion*
>   *is a sun-heart kaleidoscope*
>   *and I have lost myself*
>   *and been found*
>
>   *been drawn into the gold*
>   *and burned there*
>   *alive*

here he comes with his stories
of the shifting shape of coal-fire red
but I tell you
I have *been* there
and I *know*

shaman (to the hunt)

the one who was the bull
who was the snake
sheds his skin
then rises up renewed
once more

he wears the hide
that was buffalo
adjusts the mask
to become deer

through the snout of wolf
the eyes of owl
he knows this is the time
and through the feet of bear
begins to move

> *a primordial stuttered step*
> *a neolithic grunted howl*
> *a paleolithic reverence*
> *a neanderthal offering of self*

the new man becomes complete
as he sways
to the crash
and the pounding
to the thrash
of a beaten drum

he steps onto the clouds
cries a song to the sky and the wind
and the beasts below

> *moon is full*
> *moon is high*

tonight he rides outside himself
among the beasts he has called
to the sacrifice again

ki-aiy-aiy-ay
ki-aiy-aiy ay-aiy-aiy-aiy-ay
ki-aiy-aiy-o
ki-aiy-ay aiy-aiy-aiy-aiy-o

maketh the man

she drew her hands from the pool
squeezed and shaped the mud
sang a murmur while patting the form

    la la   la-la-la la la

and moulded a small man-figure
that she sat down beside her

she gave him a mouth —
smiling —
and two eyes
then breathed on him once

breathed again

    la la   la-la-la la la

it was no surprise at all
when he moved his arms
clambered up to stand wobbling
on the legs she'd made
especially for him

the first word that he spoke
was her name

    la-la-la

and that was the song they sang together

    la-la la-la-la

when the call rang out for supper
she put him down
back in the water he came from

she would return later
to squeeze and shape the mud
and breathe him into life
again

    la

    la la
    la-la

    la-la-la-la

Joseph Cambell - Mythology

a call: a dance: here again: gone

she plucks on the strings
of the lapis-lined harp
fills the air
with the song of summoning

first the right hand
then the left

she plays
through long hours of darkness

and the call wells up
transforming to joy
when a slender hint of crescent
becomes the lunar form
returned

a greater presence each night
she plays until the full
when the harp is abandoned
for dance

with a downward thrust
she stamps life into the earth
then a kick high into the air
for release

while all the time —
unmarked —
the peak slowly passes
and black night again creeps near
to steal glory

joy becomes
a melancholy thing
the dance
a confused reel
bereft of purpose

until all that remains
is an emptied husk
with a yearning desire for a song
to pluck on her harp
the summons
again

rolling

endless rolling
I fall down from the heights
to the plains

even if I tried
I could not find my way
to home
again

afloat
I'm at the whim-break of a tide
that laps up against
and moves
my fragile craft and mind
that is endlessly rolling along

this is my life

the search for truth

tonight I eat the roasted meat
gifted me by the friend
who strayed from his herd
to fall beneath my spear

charred and brown
hot juices soak my beard

> *where do you come from
> beast friend*
>
> *I found you and slew you
> I cut you down
> with reverence in my heart*
>
> *but where were you
> where was your herd
> when the plain before me
> lay empty*
>
> *what caused the womb
> to open
> from what seed
> did you grow*
>
> *to which god should I kneel
> in my gratitude*

I will wear you for my cloak
you will keep your spirit through me
I will make your image upon my walls
in the red-ochre that stains my nails

> *o lord of the herd
> o sire who is the meat of life
> you have come from beyond the plains
> and I will walk with you
> when you leave*

the sound of the song

!

and there was a sound
that was a note
to begin a chord

and there was the song
that reached with its depth
to fill the void

yes the sound
was the note
was the chord
was the song

!

and the silence
that rocked the dream of evermore
in its un-ending sleep
was *not*

and then we wait

this time it is I
who am the knife
and you
my willing one

come let your face reveal
the ecstasy

and I swear that I will take you
at the cresting of that flood
while you are at your moment
of elation

I do not call you *victim*
you will come again
and next
will be my own time
to taste the blade

I will draw
the marks of sleep upon you
in red
and on myself —
the hand that slew —
then
I will lie with you upon the stone
and embrace the emptiness
while we await the morning
and the return
of the sun

within beauty

we find our god
with sounds
and names
and with pictures

we find god
wrought in beaten gold
and in fine silver

we find *the one*
in all the things we name
beautiful

for the daily bread

cut him slice him
pass him around
put the pieces
in the ground

when he is buried
god will know
and send the rain
to make food grow

a slice of light

as he sat at the grindstone
honing an edge in the perpetual gloom
he thought to himself

> *this world of darkness had need*
> *for something more*

with the knife at his side
he inspected the harvest of grown things
selected the ripest of the golden squash
then sliced free a disk

with his face bathed
in the glorious yellow glow
he nodded satisfaction
and threw the orb spinning
high into the sky

twilight was banished
day created

> *there*

he said

> *let that golden slice reside up there*
> *in the sky*
> *and show us all*
> *what there is in this world*
> *to see*

the higher crafts

she wondered
while unpicking the wool
seated in her work-chair
beside the fire

wondered if perhaps
it was *herself*
that was becoming unraveled
shook her head to clear the thought
and started re-balling the yarn

each evening she would settle in
to start the pattern anew
needles clacking in double time

      tat-tat tat-tat tat-tat

and the shape would form rapidly
for she had skill at the craft

but no matter what variation she tried
it still was not right
lacked a certain something
some quality of *warmth*
or a *presence*
and had to be started over again

she mused to herself
laughed aloud once to think
it was rumoured
that they'd made a woman
out of simple rib

what *tosh*

rib is fit only for cuffs and edgings
and it takes more
than an arc of gristle
to shape a body

a long night to sunrise

a man is seated at the table

in a small house
behind the sun

he is old
fingers gnarled
but he grasps tight the cogs
in his stiff bony hands
and adjusts the links
in a length of chain

sings
underneath his breath
to a time-piece rhythm

>*ah-yay ah-yay ah-yay ah*

>*ah-yay ah-yay ye-ah*

mutters to the woman beside him

>*old lady*
>*can you get a working man*
>*his cup of tea*

>*for if the sun's to rise*
>*I'll be freeing-up these cogs*
>*all night*

>*it's going to be a long slow time*
>*until morning*

the day craft

she sat at her wheel
beneath the broad sweep
of open sky

as each bright ray
reached down to touch her
and warm her while she worked
she caught it in a tender grasp
crooned quietly
and applied herself to the repetitions

warm and spin
warm and spin

as the day cooled
ray upon ray
she shawled herself against the chill
and spun
until the last

until the night

and then the loom

clack clack
and *clack* again

warp
weft

the shuttle flew
she wove for morning

for another rising
of the sun

Joseph Cambell - Mythology

the tower of contemplation

all through his life
he worked with the mud
the black silt that came anew
each year the river flooded
and grew the rich food he depended on

with the grey powdered clay
that baked hard in the dry months
and turned the road into a slippery slither
when the sometime rains
fell across the country

he studied it in the walls of his hut
an adobe mixture with strands of straw
visible on the smooth surface

and all through his life
he gazed up at the heavens
the peerless blue of summer
unblemished by any wisp of cloud

the golden sun that drove the seasons
and burnt his back as brown as coffee
a harsh master that punished all
when it prevented the wet season

then at night the stars
always his ritual before the sleep demanded
by his aching body
was to gaze for long moments
up at the points and shapes and designs

and on a day like any other
but *un*like them all
he began to work with the mud
to dig it and water it mix it with straw
and form it into workable bricks

brick after brick he formed
for a long season
stacked together while they dried
he made more until he reached
a mighty number

one morning he laid a first row of bricks
in the form of a circle
and then another
rising up from the ground
he built a scaffold and laid more bricks

inside
a staircase to follow his tower
around and around higher and higher

he built until his tower grew slender
and could accept no more bricks
and here he built a platform of timber
and placed a mat

in the night now
he dreamt of his tower and its height
how a man could rise
literally
through the boon of his own labour
to be close to heaven

in the cold dark
before the first trace of light
he would slowly climb the steps of his creation
until he could kneel on his mat
cast his eyes to the stars
and await the first colour touch
on the eastern horizon

sometimes his voice might be heard faintly

> *ahhh ahhh*
> *it is good*
>
> *it is good*

Joseph Cambell - Mythology

through passion (hey!)

the world was built
from passion

the dancers rose
up out of the centre
red-sheathed and entwined
emerging smooth
from the living orange

to swirl around each other
blended in motion

> *ta-ra-ta-ta*
> *tara-ta-tata-ta-ta*
> *ta-ra-ta-ta*

he bent her backwards
her hair fell low

in it's wake a forest

> *ta-a-ra-ta-ta*

they kicked out together
and where their feet touched
a mountain

> *tarara-ta-tatata*

they came together
burning stares into each others eyes
then up

> *ta-ra*

the cosmos

ta-ra-ta-ta
tara-ta-tata-ta-ta
ta-ra-ta-ta

she began to stamp
he too
a tattoo rhythm rippling out
rippling in

ta-ra-ta
hey!
tara-ta-ta-ta-ta
hey! hey!

and then to splash
in and out of the moving waters
and kicking up into the sky

ta-ra-ta-a

where it grew into cloud
then fell down again

and the air grew cooler
the dance slowed down

so very slow

without the heat
they are not fire
after all

but once . . .

they woke the world
through passion

oracle midwife (cubist morning:picasso day)

his middle eye is focused
on something still to come
his other one is watching
us

with one ear he's listening
the other is not here
his lips are murmuring whispers
of what will be

what will be . . .

of what has been

a gesture
an incantation
tics and twitches
and shouts and screams

birthing rites have ever been sung
this way

when the sun has passed it's height
his trembling fades
a slump into the corner speaks eloquently
and the day he made has died

beneath the creeping shade
evening steals colour
away from the light
but he is not dead

no it's only the passing of a time
and he will rise again
unfix his eyes and let the palsy dance
resume his arms and legs

to wake up the morning
again

cracking the code

I think I understand the philosophers
better than before

a is to *b* as *c* is to *x*
and that is the point
when my feet raise me
into the air

there is no *subject-object* idea
there is no *you*
or *me*

there is only *us*
in a state of oneness
like an *aum*

just like an *aum*

and if I've got it right and
thou
art that
and *that*
is *bliss*
then
here we are

and no wonder
everything goes to shit
when there's disruption
and we have to bring otherness
back to ground

yes
schopenhauer said it quite clearly
and
it's no bloody wonder
at all

In a Foreign Tongue

In a Foreign Tongue

Politika of the Pipples

Winner of the Dan O'onnell Poetry Readings prize for a poem incorporating the phrase 'who will be left to play the post-apocalyptic violin' – August 2001.

So! *Frenk!*
You are *skippi* or *Evropski* — from Europe?
Da, ja isto — me too — but you have lived here all life, yes?
I am only here few years.

What do you do? Oh, poet!
We have many poet in my country,
is long tradition, is very *politik*, you know?
Telling *pipples istina* — the truth.
What you write?
What? *Kako to?* How can you no be writing *politik*
if you are poet?

Frenk, *slušsaj* — listen to me
when I was *mlad čovjek* — a young man
my country communist was. Eh, bastards.
We *pipples* no can say nothing, you know?
Every place bastard informer has, schools must learn
bloody communist. *Je bempti*, bastards!
It was poetry, it was stories, this was all we have,
za sjeećanju — for remembering.
You know this communist bastards,
they want us to forget
who am we, who we have been, yes.
It was stories, *pjesme* – songs — you know,
they tell us, they tell our children, *Frenk*. They say
why do we exist, why are we proud, why we suffer.

Communisti, they make the smell, *sve prljavo* —
everything dirty.
They are loud, like orchestra drums and *trumpeti*,
make noise too big for cello *i* violin, but is important -
if you have music ear — is important to listen
for little bit that violin.
Sometimes when big noise bastard
is taking *zrak* — the breath —
sometimes you can hear him.

This *communisti* was apocalypse for my *pipples*, you know?
Was poets, songs keep my *pipple* alive
inside their hearts where this bastards cannot touch.

Pa tako, jedan dan — so, one day, all sudden,
communisti are gone — pht! — no more.
But this violin, this poetry is playing after apocalypse.
Everyone can hear him now. *Prekrasno* -
is very beautiful — and, is sound of our hearts.

So, *Frenki* boy, you are *politik*, yes.
You are violin in orchestra of big freedoms, yes *Frenk*, you.
Is not bullshit, is poets who will be left to play this -
kako se ka"že — how you say him — is poets
who will be left to play the post-apocalyptic violin.

Yes Frenk, you are the *politika* of the *pipples*.

Moisture in My Kitchen

kišića pada na moj krov
sad je zima tu
sve je normalno

stojim i gledam napolje iz moj kuhinja
i mislim da sam
i ja možda malo vlažan

a little rain is falling on the roof
it is winter here now
it is natural

I stand and look outside from my kitchen
and think that
I too may be a little damp

the first love

You love your country, *Frenki*? This place where you grow up, become man? Yes, I love her plenty, too, but she is not my number one love. That one is far away, over land and sea. Maybe more over sky today, but when I come here was everyone in the big boat. *Avion* was not so much then.

I still think of her like home, you know? She is not my home no more, but that is how I call her.

When I was little boy, we have the big war. Then, after, we have *communisti*. It was then, when I grow up to man, I decide to leave her. I love her, you know, but I have to leave. The *communisti režim* was too strong, they choke me up to the neck, nearly. So, I go. I come to Australia.

Frenk, sometimes I think of her too much, still. Is like I have hole in my heart, but here is my living. Here is me. Sometimes, this is very hard.

Communisti is gone now. Is free much more, but is not mine. My love is from long time back, and these new ones, what they can do for man like me? Nothing. Is just new *re"zim* instead old one. I am now *Australski* strange-man, with heart for here, and heart back with lover from too many old years gone.

Yes, can be hard, sometimes.

Day of Peace, Dojdi Mi

>   *dojdi mi, dojdi*
>   *dojdi, ako je samo za jedan dan*
>   *molim malo mir, molim ja*
>   *dojdi mi*

a single day of peace
doesn't come so easy
escape isn't there at the moment
when I really need to go

little prayers don't comfort
no matter what words I say
and the bigger asks
are out of reach

>   *samo za jedan dan, mir*
>   *dojdi mi*

just for a day peace,
come to me

intra-city migration

ai em not particular heppy here
yu no
is new plaice for me ent ai do not laik him tu much
is very kuld all time
no heater to maik warm
ai em shiver ver' much in dai ent in every nighttimes
but yu no
wat ken ai do
ai mus' sumwere livink be
so tis plaice is o-kai ontil wuan dai
ai better sumtink can find
yu no

ai kom here from long way away
from malvern
near very big shoppink plaz
on uder site melborn city

ai kom here becoz me and wooman
ken no more togeder be
ai kennot wat she wonts be doink
ent she mus' learn now to do dis tinks for self
saim me here
ai mus' now how to kooking unnerstent
yu no

is liddle bit sed for me
dis tink
but what ken a men do
sumtime is bes' he mus' go

so ai move here to dis kuld shit-hip house jedan
wit holes all everywhere in rouf
maik it so rain only straik me
wit ever' sevent droppink

is o-kai
ai fin' sumting better wuan dai

In a Foreign Tongue

a tough country

you know
this one was hard country, *Frenk*
back in days when I was work in mental asylum
I am helper to nurses them days
in ward for old people
some of them was very bad
wetting and dirty all time, *phooy!*
and mind not all here, you know
but some was ok

there was this one man, Fred
he was good like the gold
every day after dinner in evening
we sit down play cards
he was good player for little bit time
then he get cranky
but he pretty good like you and me

anyway
one day we all get on bus
we all go for outing
all the best patients and the staff
we go for *Chil-tren* races

believe me *Frenk*, when I tell you
it was so much beer into that bus
I never could believe
box and box, all beer
and
the patients is supposed to be no drinking
ha!
this was for staff only

well
we go, no worries
plenty beer for every staff in bus
everybody happy
songs singing

we get to races
is lovely
very green, nice tree everywhere
horse running gidd-i-up
lovely, you know

the nurse-man who is boss this day
Stephen
he say like this
we going home soon
I think all the good men patients
they can be having one, two beers
ok, we give them beers

Frenki, the man Fred what I telling you
he get beer and he go
woof *jedan*, woof *dva*
two beers is gone just like that
and now he look hungry
he want more beer
but no can have, so
he get angry,
not so nice this time
oh he shout every you-bastard at us
you know

ok, never mind
five minutes later he be quiet
all calm
he go sleep in bus on way home
no problem

I look at him, *Frenk*
he has dark on front of pants
joj
he is wet pants, on seat for the bus
everywhere

start bloody bus
go home

In a Foreign Tongue

oh yes, I remember *Chil-tren* racing, too much
but do you know, *Frenk*
what I am thinking that time
I am thinking
this Australia must be bloody tough country
when man who cannot hold the beer
have to go to live in mental home
is bloody tough, mate

you get me next beer
I go to little boy room for minute

materinski jezik — the mother tongue

Frenk, tell me, why you not use you mother language some more, hmmm?

You speak *Australski*, yes, but this is not you mother tongue. You mother tongue is *Hrvatski*, you call him Croatia, no? That is language you was born with and you papa and mama speak him, why you no speak him more, why always *Australski, Australski*?

Yes, *Frenk*, of course you not too good speaking him, if you don't get *praksu*, the practice, how you can be speaking him good?

True, even you mama and you papa mix him up now, with the *Australski* and the *Hrvatski sve* in *jedan*. And your *Onkel od* Germany, too? What he do? Oh, he mix *Deutsch* with the *Hrvatski*? Ha!

This *mjeshanje* of languages is no good. I think *svako*, eh, everyone, should speak mother language proper, no more mixing-ups.

Frenki, you go now to you grandmother, to you *oma*, and you speak her and you listen to proper *Hrvatski* speaking – this beautiful language! Maybe is something you can be learning.

What you saying, *Frenk*? *Oma* is mixing *Australski*, too?

Oh, *joj*!

coffee with sweet sugar (every morning)

ja imam šećer u moju kafu

I have sugar in my coffee

šećer da je tako malo slatko

sugar so that it is a little sweet

svako jutro čim se sunce dize u plavo nebo

every morning when the sun raises itself
into the blue sky

jedna mala kafa ja i šećer   slatko

one small coffee I   and sugar   sweet

encouragement for a new image

Eh, *Frenki*, you cut you beard off. What for you do that?

You want to catch girly with you clean face, with you beautiful looks, huh? Ah, I know this things.

In my country we don't have the beards too much. We have the *brkovi*, the moustaches but *brada*, not so much. Men mostly is not liking the *brijanje*, so we have the moustache and little bit rough face. That way we handsome, good looking boys. Look little bit tough, but very gorgeous, you know?

In my town, all the girls like the *brke* when I wear them as young man, oh yes. Is good to be young and with the big *brkovi*.

So, what? You think man with *brada* look too old? *Možda*, this is possible. *Frenk*, you must ask the girls, the cure, only they can tell us this for true.

Evo, vidi ova tu, look, is girl here, we tell her question, see what she is thinking.

Frenk, slušaj, please be quiet for minute jedan, I asking her.

Escuse me, miss, you can please tell me, you see my friend? You like him without beard, or you think him better if cover up?

You think he good looking? You like your man with clean face, for better kiss? Oh, ok, I tell him. And you, you are having good time? You like drink with me and clean shaving man? No? Ok, I only asking.

See *Frenki*, she like you with no beard. *Ma, je*, she say you look very good. Eh, why you not ask her for drink? I try, but she no like me so much. You are beautiful now, you do much better. *Idi*, go, ask her for drink, I wait here for if she say no.

Pa, idi ve'č! What you waiting?

Sretna New Godina, Frenki

In a Foreign Tongue

Sretna nova godina, Frenki, sretna nova. Happy New Year. What kind of year you have in this one you finish now? *Kako ye ti bilo*, huh?

Oh, *izgleda da si* — eh, looks like you have change you life altogether very big. You live alone, by self now, yes? *Pa, ja isto*, me too. Is not so bloody-bad, you know? Man can think better *kad je on malo sam*, when he is all alone for little bits. Woman is not everything, you know?

When I first was coming here to Australia, alone I am for seven years. I am working in bush, saving moneys, drink little bits when comes the Friday night. One packet *cigaret-e, samo svaki drugi dan* — only every second day. I am *sam* – alone. Is very hard this, I am *mladi čovjek* — a young man then, I am ready for *zivot i zena* — whole of life and for woman too, you know, all at same time, you understand what I am saying? I am young, not afraid nothing.

I look at this *skippi* boys I working with, they funny strange bastards, you know, sometimes they *glup* — stupid, sometimes ugly, like yuk, you know, but every one can get girl. At this time, they have the dances *svaku subotu* — on every Saturday night, in the little town, in the hall. I am not too bad looking in these days and sometimes I ask this girls for dance, but, too much they laugh me in face. Ok, *tako je, ja razumjem to* – that is how it is, I can understand.

Sometimes, in these days, girl will look to me, *Frenki*, and I think she want to say, yes, let us dance, little bit, but she is with *grupa* – with her friends, and I can see she know her friends not agree is good idea she to dance with me. So she look away, shake head, no, she don't want to dance me. Ok.

After seven year, I have money, little bits. I can buy house *crim-brik* in city, in *Brun-es-wick*, or in *Santa Al-bans*, maybe *Keelor-r*, you know. I am in good position now in world, *i ja mislim sam sebi, evo, sad je vreme* — I think, is time now. Is time I find woman for me. But big question, where to find this woman, where to go look? Could be she might be *doma, u moj stari selo* — back home in my old village, where girls all want to marry rich man from America. Could be she in Philippines. Some men, same like me, they come with nothing, work like idiot, make money. Some of this men have go to Philippines, come back with very nice girl, very good, already babies having, oh yes, this *Philippin-a's* is no worries, mate.

Or, *jedan drugi put* — one more way, I could look at the girl childs *od te nasi ljudi* – of peoples from old country living here in *Santa Al-bans*, *Keelor-r*, *Sun-e-shine*, you know. Maybe one from *Syd-e-ney*.

So I must do one of this things. What to do? I tell you what happen, but first excuse me, I must go looking for dark place on fence for moment.

You get more drinks, I finish story for you. Is beauty New Years Eve, no?

I be back, give me just minute *jedan*.

scribble artist

Eh, Frenki, you are with you computer again? Huh!

Frenki, you think you are *nekaki* writing artist, you think you make beautiful thing with you pencil, with you paper, yes?

Huh! *slušaj Frenki*, you know nothing. You just sitting at you computer, writing, writing, you make you little story. All right, is very good, but what is this to do with art?

When I was *mali* boy, in village, was man who make pictures. He can draw you anything you ask, but, is never look like what he starting with. He make it twisty, he make it stand on head, he make it opposite. He doing all sorts, so that picture is, but at same time, is not. You know?

When this man is looking at thing what he want to draw, he is making change *u glavi*, inside he head, you understand? So what he put in this canvas is like synthetic picture, you know, what I am saying?

Yes, yes, is synthesised by he in brain. That what I mean.

What he begin is only model, what he finish is art.

You get this people today, they take picture, *click*. They put him on easel, *tsank*. They draw him exact what they see.

Phooy!

This is not art. Art is when you take him out from somewhere deep in you head.

Which one is you *Frenki*, artist, or just pretty scribble-boy, hmm?

Which one you?

a problem with stinky writing

What for is you problem, *Frenk*?

You acting funny, like you not happy, like maybe you afraid. What you got to be afraid?

Ah, someone say something, say what you writing is little bit stinky, huh? And what? You think what he say is true? You don't know. Ok.

Frenki, tell me, is everyone say, '*You write stinky poem*'? No.

Is someone say, *'eh, Frenk, you better write you poetry on toilet, is only good for that.'* No.

Is someone say sometime, '*Frenki, this one is very beautiful.*' Yes.

Uhuh.

Frenki, what you want? Everybody be in love with you? You want this?

No.
Yes.
Maybe.
No.

Ha.

Slušaj ti, moj sinko, you are lucky man. You sometime can make the specijalni *međik in you pen*, the beautiful story for somebody to listen, to say, oh, this one is exactly for me. Everybody all time no, somebody sometime, yes.

You are too, too much lucky for this *Frenki*, this, this present to you. You better start be happy and stop you sooky business.

Go, *napisaj si nešto*. Write something, only this time, you try make him good, for change, ok?

I see you later.

a message to Christina

Hello?

Hello?

Oh.

Christina? Ah, *dobro*.

Christina, hello. This, you name, is very beautiful, you know? *Moja draga mama* also was named Christina, only we say him *Kristina*, is spell little bit *njemački*, because family mine is one time German.

What I was saying? Oh, yes. Christina, I want to tell you this *Frenki* is good boy, (he man, you know, but I always say he boy because he not so old like me).

Frenki is good boy, but he worry too much is he write good today, is this one for rubbish, what somebody is saying. He sometimes silly in this way, you know?

I want ask you, and all friend of you, make sure he don't believe too much that this is for worry. The poet and the poet writing – the *pjesme i riječi* — is very beautiful and is big present from the soul. He need to be understanding that this is enough. If everyone is not happy, this is little sad thing, but words *i pjesme* is still very much beautiful.

Christina, please, you and you friend make sure he understand this.

Ok? Good.

do vidjenja, Kristina, do vidjena, was nice speaking you.

in translation: we should leave

Sada mi dojdeš?

Koji vrijeme je ovo stići doma?

She saying to him:
Now you here? What time this is, to be arrive home?

Ti i tvoja neculturna banda! Jel niste znali koji vrijeme je već prošlo?

She say:
You and you no-culture band, eh ... group ... of friend.

Do you not know what time is past?

Evo ti, vataj ako oćeš jesti!

She say:
Here, you catch if you want to eat something. Careful *Frenk*, for you jacket. Oh, sorry. We clean later.

I ti? Šta ti brbljaš? Zasto si ti tu u ovaj vrijeme? Jel nemaš sam svoj dom? Huh? I ko je ovaj stebom? Neki novi?

She saying to me, now:
And what you babbling, why you here this time, you no have home for you-self, and who is this new one with you?

Ja ču ti dat novi jedan, samo ti čekaj!

She say: I show you new one, just wait you!

Frenk, I think it better we leaving she and she husband now.

Quickly before she come back. Quickly . . .

Sorry *Frenk*.

She is . . . what is words. . . too little toleration. Is better we leave *they* now. I take you to small *gostionica* is open late.

We talk more in that one. I sing you song from *moj stari dom.*

one more chances

> *Kad ti nešto tako dojde*
> *Frenki,*
> *nemoj čekat, sinko moj,*
> *samo nemoj ti čekat.*

Frenk, when I was young man, I think I tell you this before, *tsure*, the girls, they always like me too much.

I am beautiful young man, them days, very *handso*, you know?

I walk all time like man who own whole street. I make the special *zrak* to follow wherever I must go.

How can the *tsure* not be loving me too much? Is not possible.

But, you know, *jedan dan* I turn, look at me and, *oh hoh*, I am not young no more.

Not so beautiful.

I am nearly old like my *otata*, with the *veliki trbuv*, big hair in *moj nos*. Make snore like pig when I sleeping.

Not so good for the *tsure* no more, huh?

I say, *baš me briga*. I don't care. I am for me and this is ok.

Who is concern I am alone? Not me, *Frenki* boy, not me.

~

You see this picture on wall *Frenki*? She is beautiful, this one, yes? Who you believe her be? My daughter? My niece?

No, *Frenki*. She is my girlfriend. She and me go to movie, we holding hands in street. We are happy and we together like the lovebirds.

What you mean she is too young? You are insult to me. Is good job you are *moj prijatelj* or I don't want to tell you things no more.

She is girlfriend. She is young woman. She don't care I am *nekaki stari dino-sor*.

She say she see me like young man. Still beautiful only better. She think I am smart one, too.

Is good, that one, yes?

Anyway, *Frenki*, I don't tell you my loving-life story. I tell you something different. *Slušaj*, when you get you chance, you one-time second chance,

Frenki, you must take him. You must take him and hold him. You don't let go.

You never too old, *Frenki*, to take this one more chance.

Take him *sinko moj*. Just you take him.

buying cucumbers

djuro i djuka were *bratici* –

it means little brothers (cousins really)

they were raised in neighbouring villages
where they grew to be men
did their time in the army
started their families

both emigrated to germany
for awhile
had their second children –
hamburg and bremmen
then came to australia
to live

~

djuka lived in the city
santa ahlbuntz
with so many others
from the old country

they were assembly workers at ford

or on the biscuit line
at the rowntree chocolate factory

running the local milek-bar

boiler-making
at the sunshine harvester factory
or at massey-ferguson tractors

talking *hrvatski* (croatian) with a pole

speaking german with a lat

~

meanwhile *djuro* landed at *bitchwort*
a small town in the sticks

In a Foreign Tongue

talking hand-sign
with the boss of the sawmill

stumbling phrases at the butchers
to get a recognisable cut of meat

keeping the old language for home
after work

learning wog english to get *kruv* –
bread –
for the table

~

djuka said:
it was bulla-shit

djuro said:
ne to je istina
it is true

djuka said:
he could get *makar shta* . . .

whatever he wanted

djuro said:
no
nije to jednostavno u selo
it's different in a small town

djuka said:
hajde
come on
da vidimo
let's see

djuro said:
okai

~

>   *escoos mi*
>   *ai wont koo-kom-berrs*
>   *plis*

'ey?

pointing to a shelf

>   *ai wont koo-kom-berrs*

sorry
what do you want?

>   *koo-kom-berrs*

george
can you help . . .

what does he want?

djuro says:
yes norm
he wants some *kew-cumbers*

norm turns around
and gets a bottle of gherkins
produce of croatia

why didn't you say so
mate?

conversation with my cousin

... and do you remember when a pig was killed and the women would make *suls*? Mainly for *Opa*, I think

It was a kind of clear savoury jelly with a few bits of trotter or knuckle in it — mostly jelly and not much meat because the meat was used in sausages and other stuff. You used to hate it didn't you? It was nearly as bad as cabbage *čuspajz*, no?

They always made *čevabčiči* when they did the pig too, no, no ... *čevabčiči* are a kind of small oblong rissole with lots of garlic, I meant those little pork-fat and bacon bits they fried to eat by the handful as a cold snack.

Čvarke, yes that's right, they were called *čvarke*.

I never really liked *bijela kobasica* — the white sausage. It was a bit better after it had been in the old laundry they used as a smokehouse at slaughter time, but the *crna kobasica* — black pudding — was a treat.

Your mum was the best at making *torte*. The layers were so thick they tasted like solid sweetness. Many an egg died in the pursuit of my happiness, I can tell you. You weren't around then, but I can still recall when I was just a few years old, at your mums wedding, they made dozens of sugar-coated coloured fruits from marzipan. They looked out of this world but tasted of rubbish, I reckon.

My favourite cake when I was a kid was made out of *mak* — poppy seeds. Yum. We need to ask *oma* about her recipe for making *peretze* – pretzels.

I think they get boiled, then baked, but I don't know the right dough to use. They had a sort of salty paste on the joins and were covered in salt crystals.

We can ask her tomorrow.

Did your mum do *kokošje noge* — chooks feet — in the soup?

Ich Liebe Dich

ich liebe dich

my uncle stopped his lady
in the middle of Melbourne
turned her around
till they were standing
with their faces close
and held her

he just said it
in a quiet voice and with a soft look
so she knew he meant it
and there was a smile
creasing the corners of her eyes
while they went a little bit shiny
and moist

standing there for a couple of moments
I tried to make myself
and the rest of the street invisible
but I don't think it really mattered much
to them

promise about a life

Eh, *Frenki*. How you go? Everything is good? *Ma je*, everything is good for me, too. Only I am sick for couple days. Not bad now.

Is ok.

What you doing, you work up in bush town now, yes? I hear this from friend. He tell me, he say, *Frenki* go to bush to do psychiatric some-bastard job.

I hear everything what you do, *Frenki* boy.

Why you not tell me you have girlfriend? Why I am last one knowing this?

Huh. When I get to see this girl? I have thing to tell her, thing she need to know about you, mister *Frenki*? Ha ha!

No, no, I only joking. You know I like it to know you are happy, and you have lovely woman. She is beautiful, yes? Yes. This is very good.

Ah, Frenk, Frenk. Is funny life this one sometimes, you know. My friend from home, he is living in *Deutschland*. Is lovely man, but has very hard life. This woman what he marries first time, she is little bit not together in head, you know?

I visit him one time, nearly she drive even me crazy, but, he is good man and they stay together and he looks after she and son until boy is big to look after self.

When my friend is not so young, maybe *šezdeset godina* – when he is sixty, he she not living together. They do divorce and he must something give to her for ever. This is the *Deutsch* law, you know, is hard for him, but is better.

Anyway, *Frenki*, he find young woman who love him, just like you. Couple years, five, six, they are happy, *Frenki*. And, everyone is happy, too. They make you happy, just because he she have the *ljubav*. They are in love and make everybody smiling.

Is very sad. He is sick now. *Rak na stomak* . . . he has the cancer, and they open him for look, very soon.

Frenki, make me promise, *jedan*, please. You promise me you will be happy. You and you *žena*. Promise you don't waste no time, and don't waste your lifes.

Can you tell me that promise? We nobody got time for spare, *Frenk*. We got no time

sleeping tales

my father is unhappy
he says I have written
too close to home
in the telling of a story
about hotel life

he thinks I have intruded
shown too much
that the revelations
might reflect poorly on him

he has changed the place he drinks
~

and so I have promised I will search no more
for the stories that only he can tell
I will no longer pen his tales

and I will never again
seek the recipes
for *rakija*
or *slivovic*
recipes that would be a rich poetry
in the mere listing of their ingredients

will never tell the secrets
of the *'breadroom'* in the old hospital
that I found fascinating
when I was a child
with its machine that could butter bread
while it rapid-sliced the loaf
always leaving the slices right side up

and where men would sit on butter-boxes
on a sunday afternoon
drinking until they fell
only to be discovered by the boss
instantly dismissed

except for the man
who slid timely into the storeroom
through a connecting hatchway
and kept his job

but
I will leave them alone
I have promised my father
and I do not enjoy his displeasure

no
I will not write them
will let them lie sleeping
until my father's time is passed
and the tales themselves are dead

telephone dumplings

mutti said
Frenk you should be here
I'm making *k-nedl-e*
do you remember
what they are
dumplings for putting into chicken *supa*

sounds good ma
but what I always remember
from when I was a kid
is *šoof-nudl-e*
the yellow doughy-pastry that you used to make
into long thin ropes
by rolling it backwards and forwards fast
on your knee in the laundry

she laughed

don't be silly *Frenki*
that was a joke I did once
for you children
šoof-nudl-e are rolled on a pastry board
you funny boy

supa is ready
do you want some

I wish you were here
goodbye now

Zlata's Daughter

I met *zlatitsa* when I was young
on a visit to the old country
we held hands at the village dance
and walked evenings on the *corzo*

when I left
she gave me golden dice on a chain
and said *osjećaj me* — remember me

~

zlata is a mother now
a grandmother a survivor of war
between *croats* and *serbs*

I don't understand what the hell
they thought they were doing
to places where we went to talk and dream
and hold hands as we walked
across the *corzo* cobbles

~

zlata named her daughter *mariana*
srce moj (my heart)
grew up an imitation *americanka*
but in a landscape painted small
with *dinars* instead of dollars
she met *dejan* on the *corzo* before a dance

mariana couldn't help herself	fell for a *serb*
and *dejan* chose wrong blood	*mariana* a croat

there was hatred in the village
for kids like that

betrayers of kin
consorts of the enemy
damn fool pacifists

In a Foreign Tongue

he should have shaved her hair
put her out on the street

she should have cut his throat
in the middle of the night

~

I met zlata's daughter
her dejan
and their child
at a migrant place in dandenong

she told me it was better here
australians haven't learned to wear
the look that gets etched into faces
from living with war

she said she was a little lonely
no-one from home comes to visit
but they leave messages on the outside wall:

> *no place here for a croatian-serb*
> *no place here for a serbian-croat*
> *no place here for people like you*
> *go away go away become invisible*

she said they would leave in the morning
to go to a far away town
where no-one knows where they come from
who they are
what they are
leave the war behind them
and find a place where their child will grow
without an accent
without a heritage
without knowing hate

~

when I last saw her
zlata's daughter
was wearing golden dice
on a necklace
struggling with a new language
full of strange words
and keeping up a job
through difficult early times

I picture her now in my minds eye
walking with *dejan* and their daughter
on a dusty australian corzo
in a small town she calls *moje osloboɭenje*

my escape to freedom

After Words

Index of Poems

A

about thunder and lightning 113
a call: a dance: here again: gone 189
a crimson in the apples (Crimson Rosella: Platycercus elegans) 145
a garden page 175
a glorious whirly and home-roast beans 88
a knowledge of the red 184
a last vestige of magic 10
a letter to the royal society 101
a liquidautumn poem 153
a little (move) 74
all in a day 139
a long night to sunrise 199
a message to Christina 225
an air holder 119
an aspara-guy song 83
and again a day 163
and then we wait 194
a problem with stinky writing 224
a quick latte (a long black) 110
as flowers strewn 129
a short statement from the latest arrival 134
a slice of light 197
at Gloria Jean's 56
a tough country 215

B

Belvedere 59
best apple 165
breeze and leaf 55
buccaneers 144
building 67
buying cucumbers 230

C

certain people 168
chin-chin christmas 102

coffee with sweet sugar (every morning) 219
conversation with my cousin 233
counting the universal number by heart 75
cracking the code 206
cruising the cat 118
cry green 116

D

dash slap 39
Day of Peace, Dojdi Mi 213
decisive pastorale 6
demonstrating dreary 46
dirty walk 115
dividing the labour 21
diving in the petrified sea 84
dog bats (for the best spot) 125
dream land 80
dry drowning 162

E

encouragement for a new image 220
everyday changing 106

F

feeling the arrival 104
for the daily bread 196
for the (rockfall) record 90
full and empty 45

G

getting on (I said getting on) 5
giggling the ivories 97
good cake 166
gregorian cats 58
growing season 29

H

hard words 132
health gone 172
hh jesus 86

hic-atoo 35
hot koala 140
hurrah for the salt 13
hush Stanley town 123

I

Ich Liebe Dich 234
if it's really . . . 41
inadequate staves 22
incomplete winter poem 73
in johnny's hat 33
intra-city migration 214
in translation: we should leave 226

J

just shopping 27

K

kate mcgarrigle (is gone) 44
kook-ing apples 135

L

Lacking a start 60
like rain 161
living lightly 178

M

maintaining equilibrium 8
maketh the man 187
man flu 173
mary's sideboard 31
materinski jezik - the mother tongue 218
mathematics and philosophy 19
Moisture in My Kitchen 211
moo-pera 48
my career in solitaire 121
my place in nothing 117

N

not listening to a flood 108

O

old dogs 179
one more chances 228
only a four 98
on the cathedral corner 47
on the milky sea 62
on the way 39
on the winter wire 70
oracle midwife (cubist morning\
  picasso day) 205

P

painting the liquid amber - an autumn day in May 154
pitter-patter 120
plays pictures 26
Politika of the Pipples 209
promise about a life 235

R

Radiance after 16
reflection at the start (of a croissant) 149
reflection (requiem) 51
rolling 191
rooster morning 126

S

sacred priest 43
scarlet robin on guard duty 155
scribble artist 223
shaman (to the hunt) 185
since I stopped 87
sleeping tales 237
solo 164
sourcing a recipe 37
Sretna New Godina, Frenki 220
s-s-s-strength 141
stars of the in-crowd 12

storm alone 180

T

taking possession 65
telephone dumplings 239
term end 176
that kind 42
the a-philosopher 112
the boy bands of palestine 24
the day craft 200
the first lord's song 183
the first love 212
the good day 64
the higher crafts 198
the hunter 81
the light (I) 61
the loquat flower:the frost:the winter 151
the love poem for you 152
the memory-keepers of april 20
theme song 34
the moon concedes in three parts 128
the return 85
the search for truth 192
The season of waiting 14
the simple life 28
the sound of the song 193
the tower of contemplation 201
The way in which Barbara can be likened to a particular kind of goat. 130
the woodshed has a floor 167
things they don't describe too well (at all) 122
through passion (hey!) 203
to a tree 143
to start the day 17
to the desert in pursuit 49
trios 169
tune today 72

U

un-bounded 78
universe smiles 23

un-rushing 69

W

warmer on the verandah 156
warm weather 171
water level 174
weighing nothing 127
what the tiler saw 18
when the man went inside 76
Whirley-gigging the coffee 92
wild winter 68
winter numb 157
with a view to the sweet-grass 103
within beauty 195
work benign 170
world tour 147
wren-cen-tralia 177

Z

Zlata's Daughter 240

Author Information

Frank Prem has been a storytelling poet since his teenage years. He has been a psychiatric nurse through all of his professional career, which now exceeds forty years.

He has been published in magazines, online zines, and anthologies in Australia, and in a number of other countries, and has both performed and recorded his work as spoken word.

He lives with his wife in the beautiful township of Beechworth in North East Victoria, Australia.

Connect with Frank

Find Frank at his website www.FrankPrem.com, or through Social Media online at Facebook, X (Twitter), Instagram and YouTube.

Other Published Works

Free Verse Poetry

Small Town Kid (2018)
Devil In The Wind (2019)
The New Asylum (2019)
Herja, Devastation - With Cage Dunn (2019)
Walk Away Silver Heart (2020)
A Kiss for the Worthy (2020)
Rescue and Redemption (2020)
Pebbles to Poems (2020)
The Garden Black (2022)
A Specialist at The Recycled Heart (2022)
Ida: Searching for The Jazz Baby (2023)
From Volyn to Kherson (2023)
Alive Is What You Feel (2023)
White Whale (2024)
Pilgrim Volume 1 - Illustrated by Leanne Murphy (2024)
A Poetry Archive Volume 1 (2024)
A Poetry Archive Volume 2 (2024)
A Poetry Archive Volume 3 (2024)
A Poetry Archive Volume 4 (2024)

Picture Poetry/Spoken Image

Voices (In The Trash) (2020)
The Beechworth Bakery Bears (2021)
Sheep On The Somme (2021)
Waiting For Frank-Bear (2021)
A Lake Sambell Walk (2021)
A Few Places Near Home (2023)
The Cielonaut (2024)

What Readers Say

Small Town Kid

A modern-day minstrel. Highly recommended.
—A. F. (Australia)

Small Town Kid is a wonderful collection.
—S. T. (Australia)

Devil In The Wind

Trust me, this book will stay with you. Bravo!
—K. K. (USA)

Moving, beautiful, and terrible. I was left with a profound sense of respect, as well as a reminder that we should never take for granted every precious every moment of life.
—J. S. (South Africa)

The New Asylum

Words can't do justice to the emotional journey I travelled in (reading this collection).
—C. D. (Australia)

If I had to pick one book over the past year that has truly resonated with me, this would be it.
—K. B. (USA)

Walk Away Silver Heart

Instantly grips you by the throat in his step-by-step story of survival. Bravo!
—K. K. (USA)

Outstanding!
—B. T. (Australia)

A Kiss For The Worthy

A Celebration of Life Written in Thoughtful Bursts of Poetic Expression
—C. M. C. (United States)

With every verse, I found myself reflecting about myself, my life, and the world.
—K.

Rescue and Redemption

The passion of love in its many forms explored by one for another.
 —J. L. (United States)

I've enjoyed every word, every breath. Every moment within the life of these stories.
 —C. D. (Australia)

Sheep On The Somme

Museums and archivists take note--sell this in your gift shops, preserve it in your archives. Professors, teachers--share with your students.
 —A. R. C. (United States)

(This) book is a beautiful and graphic tribute to all those brave men and women who gave their lives for their countries between 1914 and 1918.
 —R. C. (South Africa)

Ida: Searching for The Jazz Baby

I found myself deeply moved by the presentation of Ida's elusive, illusionary life.
 —E. G. (United States)

He gives her a depth and vulnerability that the press didn't.
 — A. C. (United Kingdom

The Garden Black

Prem creates verse that illuminates our world, its experiences and history.
 —S. C. (United Kingdom)

Prem's poetry reminds that life is fragile and fleeting ... both harsh and beautiful.
 —D. G. K. (Canada)

A Few Places Near Home

The author has captured many beautiful images in this book, and is a wonderful photographer as well as a poet. This book would make a beautiful coffee table book filled with moving prose to make us ponder with gorgeous accompanying images.
 —D. K. (Canada)

www.FrankPrem.com

www.ingramcontent.com/pod-product-compliance
Lightning Source LLC
Chambersburg PA
CBHW072109110526
44590CB00018B/3374